ROUTLEDGE LIBRARY EDITIONS:
ROMANTICISM

Volume 8

TRADITION AND ROMANTICISM

TRADITION AND ROMANTICISM
Studies in English Poetry from Chaucer to
W. B. Yeats

B. IFOR EVANS

LONDON AND NEW YORK

First published in 1940 by Methuen & Co., Ltd.

This edition first published in 2016
by Routledge
4 Park Square, Milton Park, Abingdon, Oxon OX14 4RN
605 Third Avenue, New York, NY 10017

Routledge is an imprint of the Taylor & Francis Group, an informa business

© 1940 Methuen & Co., Ltd.

All rights reserved. No part of this book may be reprinted or reproduced or utilised in any form or by any electronic, mechanical, or other means, now known or hereafter invented, including photocopying and recording, or in any information storage or retrieval system, without permission in writing from the publishers.

Trademark notice: Product or corporate names may be trademarks or registered trademarks, and are used only for identification and explanation without intent to infringe.

British Library Cataloguing in Publication Data
A catalogue record for this book is available from the British Library

ISBN: 978-1-138-64537-0 (Set)
ISBN: 978-1-315-62815-8 (Set) (ebk)
ISBN: 978-1-138-19002-3 (Volume 8) (hbk)
ISBN: 978-1-138-19003-0 (Volume 8) (pbk)

Publisher's Note
The publisher has gone to great lengths to ensure the quality of this reprint but points out that some imperfections in the original copies may be apparent.

Disclaimer
The publisher has made every effort to trace copyright holders and would welcome correspondence from those they have been unable to trace.

TRADITION AND ROMANTICISM

*Studies in English Poetry
from Chaucer to W. B. Yeats*

BY

B. IFOR EVANS

ARCHON BOOKS
HAMDEN, CONNECTICUT
LONDON
1964

FIRST PUBLISHED IN 1940
REPRINTED 1964 WITH PERMISSION OF
METHUEN & CO., LTD.
IN AN UNALTERED AND UNABRIDGED EDITION

LIBRARY OF CONGRESS CATALOG CARD NUMBER: 64-11060

PRINTED IN THE UNITED STATES OF AMERICA

TO
R. W. CHAMBERS

PREFACE

Though this volume was conceived as a whole, parts of it have been delivered as lectures. A few pages have been published separately as a leading article in *The Times Literary Supplement*, and I would thank the Editor for permission to reprint them. The later chapters formed the basis of three lectures delivered at the Sorbonne in 1934: some of the matter was used in 1936 in lectures in the Universities in Peking: in 1939 most of the matter was delivered in the English School at Cambridge where, for a term, I was a visiting lecturer.

B. I. E.

Queen Mary College
 University of London
  1939

CONTENTS

CHAPTER		PAGE
I.	INTRODUCTORY	1
II.	ON THE TERMS 'ROMANTIC' AND 'CLASSICAL'	7
III.	CHAUCER TO SHAKESPEARE	23
IV.	DONNE TO MILTON	44
V.	DRYDEN AND POPE	61
VI.	THE EIGHTEENTH CENTURY	76
VII.	THOMAS GRAY AND WILLIAM BLAKE	99
VIII.	WORDSWORTH, COLERIDGE, BYRON, SCOTT	109
IX.	KEATS	129
X.	SHELLEY	139
XI.	TENNYSON AND BROWNING	156
XII.	MATTHEW ARNOLD AND THE LATER NINETEENTH CENTURY	172
XIII.	TOWARDS THE TWENTIETH CENTURY: GERARD MANLEY HOPKINS AND T. S. ELIOT	185
XIV.	W. B. YEATS AND THE CONTINUANCE OF TRADITION	201
	INDEX	209

I

INTRODUCTORY

MODERN poetry has made a break with the past, and in consequence many have turned upon the past with either contempt or disdain. Often the attack has centred upon some interpretation of the terms 'romantic' and 'romanticism', which have been used with a hostile and disparaging effect. F. L. Lucas went as far as to name a volume of criticism, *The Decline and Fall of the Romantic Ideal*. Mario Praz in *The Romantic Agony*,[1] a remarkable study of erotic sensibility in romantic literature, left the impression that he had been traversing a territory fantastic, perverse, and obscene. Earlier, T. E. Hulme, viewing the romantics more generally and philosophically, wrote with unqualified condemnation: 'They had been taught by Rousseau that man was by nature good, that it was only bad laws and customs that had suppressed him. Remove all these, and the infinite possibilities of man would have a chance. . . . Here is the root of all romanticism: that man, the individual, is an infinite reservoir of possibilities.' He found that the romantic tradition had run dry, yet the critical attitude of mind, which demands romantic qualities from verse still survived. 'I object',

[1] The English translation of *La carne, la morte e il diavolo nella letteratura romantica*, Florence, 1925.

he wrote, 'even to the best of the romantics. I object still more to the receptive attitude.'[1] The American 'humanists' had reached the same position. Irving Babbitt's *Rousseau and Romanticism* was published in 1919, a year of too many preoccupations for its immediate or adequate reception in England. Babbitt had his own conceptions of tradition, and of a cultural and moral order. Though these belonged to American rather than to European controversy, his long and insistent attack on romanticism is the ultimate source of much in contemporary debate. While his conclusions were to apply to America, his illustrations and the development of his concepts arose from his study of French literature. He never indicates how far the generalizations drawn from French literature are to be applied elsewhere. From England, he seems to choose isolated examples, which adjust themselves to his argument, without considering whether the whole tradition of our poetry may not differ from that of France.

By his influence on T. S. Eliot, Babbitt has been largely responsible for the revival of 'classical' and 'romantic' as contrasting terms: the classical had 'a general nature, a core of normal experience', the product of the *esprit de finesse* in Pascal's definition. From this central reference to normal experience derived the doctrine of imitation, and from imitation in turn the doctrines of probability and decorum. T. E. Hulme had also affirmed a similar conception of the classical: 'man is an extraordinarily fixed and limited animal, whose nature is absolutely constant. It is only by tradition and organization that anything decent can

[1] *Speculations*, ed. by Herbert Read, 1936.

be got out of him.' T. S. Eliot helped to increase the sense of a conflict between 'classical' and 'romantic' by a phrase in the introduction in 1928 to an early volume, *For Lancelot Andrewes*. He spoke of himself as 'classicist in literature, royalist in politics, and Anglo-Catholic in religion'. Eliot obviously experienced some unhappiness in using these terms. 'I am quite aware', he wrote, 'that the first term is completely vague, and easily lends itself to clap-trap; I am aware that the second term is at present without definition, and easily lends itself to what is almost worse than clap-trap, I mean moderate conservatism; the third term does not rest with me to define.' Later, Eliot modified the phrasing, fearing that it might be misleading, but that the attack on romanticism remains can be seen by his republication in 1932 of *The Function of Criticism*,[1] with its assertion that the difference between 'Classicism' and 'Romanticism' is the difference 'between the complete and the fragmentary, the adult and the immature, the orderly and the chaotic'.

This modern use of the terms, with the consequent disparagement of the 'romantic', has led to an unyielding conflict in criticism which has affected judgments on the whole past of our literature. Seldom have so many great names, or whole generations of writers, been dismissed with such summary disapproval. It is almost as if the absolute oppositions of party goverment had lodged themselves upon criticism. For the attack has led some defenders of romanticism to speak out with equal severity. A. E. Housman's reputation as a great Latinist obscured the fact that in his lecture on *The Name and Nature of Poetry* he was affirming aggressively

[1] Originally published in 1923.

a romantic position: 'there is', he wrote, 'also such a thing as sham poetry, a counterfeit deliberately manufactured and offered as a substitute. In English the great historical example is certain verse produced abundantly and applauded by high and low in what for literary purposes is loosely called the eighteenth century—the period lying in between Samson Agonistes in 1671 and the Lyrical Ballads in 1798, and including as an integral part and indeed as its most potent influence the mature work of Dryden.' Herbert Read in a suggestive revaluation of the terms 'romantic' and 'classical' reached a conclusion almost as arbitrary in its relation to the past of literature. Poetry which is 'organic' begins, he suggests, with Chaucer and finds its 'final culmination in Shakespeare. It is contradicted by most French poetry before Baudelaire, by the so-called classical phase of English poetry culminating in Alexander Pope, and by the late Poet Laureate. It was re-established in England by Wordsworth and Coleridge, developed in some degree by Browning and Gerard Manley Hopkins, and in our own day by poets like Wilfred Owen, Ezra Pound, and T. S. Eliot'.[1] Apart from Browning and Hopkins, the achievements of the nineteenth century are described as 'minor tinkerings'.

The present study has been written in the belief that this controversy is misleading, and that it results from a misguided approach to the past of our poetry. The conclusions of the protagonists in the modern debate, when not governed by prejudice, are derived largely from generalizations about French and German literature, arbitrarily applied to England. The tradition of our poetry and of our criticism denies the sharp distinction

[1] *Form in Modern Poetry*, 1932.

of 'schools'. We have no 'movements' in the sense in which France had a romantic movement, and Germany a romantic school. Apart from our contemporaries, only twice in England has poetry been written to a programme; by Wordsworth and Coleridge in *Lyrical Ballads*, and by Rossetti in his application to poetry of the manifesto of the 'Pre-Raphaelite Brotherhood'. The most distinctive verse of both poets denied the principles which they set out to support. The disastrous result of the contemporary discussion is to narrow our conception of the tradition and continuity of our verse at a time when an emphasis on their existence would be valuable. The literature of the German romantic school is founded on a critical theory, and is in part its conscious illustration. In England this has no parallel, for in England there is continuity, not the break and recovery which can be seen in Germany. The conflicts in English poetry have largely been the inventions of later criticism. The alleged 'schools of poetry' have not existed in England. Changes in the conception of poetry have been usually accompanied with a tolerant attitude to the past, or at least to great writers in the past. With two or three exceptions all our major poets have found merit and enjoyment in the verse of their predecessors, even when they themselves have written in a different manner. This sense of compromise, with a consequent mingling of one form with another, has been one of the most distinctive features of our poetry.

This can be seen in any attempt to define romanticism in English poetry. So much in our verse has had elements which would answer some definition of 'romantic', and so little in our verse answers the more extreme conceptions of the term. 'Romanticism', however it be defined, does not mean the same for English poetry ás for French or German. In one way we invented the term, long after we had had the thing. We gave it to others to use with a different meaning, and then readopted it, only when it had acquired a sharpness of definition inappropriate to our poetry. Contemporary criticism is tending to obliterate the compromise from which the best in our poetry has come. Many poets who were once thought of with honour are now written down to support a theory, and the past in our poetry is reduced to something narrower than it used to be. I have attempted therefore to examine the tradition of our poetry, or rather the conception of poetry held by poets in successive centuries. It is inevitable that the function of the poet, his relationship to experience, to belief and to his audience must change from one age to another. This arises most often from causes that are deeper than any opposition of 'classical' and 'romantic'. At the same time the polarity of 'classical' and 'romantic' remains often as the most tangible way in which the problem 'the progress of poetry' can be approached. This study is not an attempt to rewrite the history of English poetry, but rather to study those artists who have modified the conception of poetry. It leads mainly to the work of those whom the poets themselves have from one generation to another judged as important, with some attention to writers who modified the outlook for poetry without achieving any work of masterly quality themselves.

II

ON THE TERMS 'ROMANTIC' AND 'CLASSICAL'

THE debate of 'romantic' and 'classical' in its older and severer forms is not worth reviving. Already the issue had long been explored in a number of contradictory ways before Alfred de Musset dealt with it with such agile wit in 1836 in his *Lettres de Dupuis et Cotonet*. Two provincial *abonnés* of a Paris *revue* had been troubled by the meaning of the word 'romanticism'. They thought that the words applied to drama only: Shakespeare was romantic because he broke the unities and sent his characters journeying to London, Athens, Alexandria, all in a quarter of an hour. Then, suddenly, to their consternation they discovered that there were romantic and classical poems, novels and even odes: 'quand nous recûmes cette nouvelle, nous ne pûmes fermer l'oeil de la nuit.' The confusions of the two provincials, of which these sleepless nights were only the first symptom, are typical of a debate longer and productive of more contradictory results than any other in literary history. Nor are these difficulties confined to de Musset's provincials. J. G. Robertson has instanced[1] one in which he was himself involved. In 1923 he had published a brilliant and

[1] *Essays and Addresses on Literature*, 1935.

learned book, entitled *Studies in the Genesis of Romantic Theory in the Eighteenth Century*, to show that the origins of romanticism in England in the eighteenth century derived ultimately from the work of a little known group of Italian critics of the *settecento*. In the same year at Bologna there appeared a work[1] by Giuseppe Toffanin suggesting that this same group of critics could be regarded as 'the heirs of the classic spirit of the Italian Renaissance'. Not only has the debate of 'classical' and 'romantic' led to contradictions, but it has proceeded to strange and unprofitable places. In its old form of the 'querelle des anciens et des modernes', to which Swift's *The Battle of the Books* was an entertaining colophon, it became strangely inverted. The advocates of the classical were there not satisfied with Homer, for Fontenelle and Perrault maintained that he needed revision to make him more regular.

Most of the definitions of 'classical' have been used, on some occasion, for the 'romantic'. Most of the definitions of 'romanticism', with some few notorious exceptions, have been used for classicism. Definition in literature, as Pater affirmed, 'becomes unmeaning and useless in proportion to its abstraction'. Romanticism differs for each European country, and the value of the term, and of the literature that can be applied to it, has varied at different periods even within a single national culture. Almost it might be said that every country has the romanticism which it deserves.

The term 'romantic' is modern, but the elements denoted by it are present long before the term is invented. The adjective, 'romantic', is far older than the noun, 'romanticism'. Its employment dates from the period

[1] *L'eredità del rinascimento in Arcadia*, Bologna, 1923.

of the popularity of the French heroical romances in England. 'Romantic' signified the quality found in fiction or in a 'romance', and since the romances usually contained far-fetched and improbable incidents, romantic came to mean something far-fetched and opposed to fact.[1] Evelyn in his *Diary* writes in 1654: 'there is also on the side of this horrid Alp a very romantic seat.' So Samuel Pepys, on the 11 March, 1667, summarized the diplomatic intrigues of the King of France and at the conclusion, wrote: 'these things are almost romantique, but yet true, as Sir H. Cholmly tells me the King himself did relate it all yesterday.' In some such sense of wild, extravagant, and improbable, 'romantic' gained increasing currency in the late seventeenth century and the early eighteenth century. Thomas Sprat in *The History of the Royal Society* used it to contrast the sober method of inquiry with vain imaginings: 'That it will cure our minds of *Romantic swelling*, by shewing all things familiarly to them, just as large as they are.' In another passage Sprat states as one of the alleged objections to learning that it makes men '*Romantic*, and subject to frame more perfect images of things, than the things themselves will bear'. In the eighteenth century, following the philosophies of Hobbes and Locke, and encouraged by the advances of experimental science, the belief gains strength that the world can be explained by reason without any resort to the mysterious or the supernatural. This can be seen in Hurd's confession

---

[1] Logan Pearsall Smith in *Words and Idioms*, 1925, has written admirably on the term 'romantic' and to him I am indebted frequently in the following pages: see also *Geschichte des Begriffes 'Romantisch' in Deutschland*, R. Ullman, and Helene Gotthard, Berlin, 1927. This volume has a useful list of sources.

that 'reason was but dawning, as we may say, and just about to gain the ascendant over the portentous spectres of the Imagination'. The phantasies, which were lost as belief, were retained as images of pseudo-belief and were designated 'romantic'.

From this distinction it is not unnatural that 'romantic' came often to be identified with 'medieval'. Heine[1] would make the two terms synonymous: 'What was the Romantic School in Germany? It was naught else than the reawakening of the poetry of the middle ages as it manifested itself in the poems, paintings, and sculptures, in the art and life of those times.' As is obvious, any such definition as applied to English literature is too narrow. Heine would restrict it even further in showing the relation of Christianity to the romantic: 'This poetry, however, had been developed out of Christianity: it was a passion-flower which had blossomed from the blood of Christ.' The indebtedness of romantic poetry to the medieval however deserves every emphasis. The attraction is seldom to any conception of the middle ages based on close study or understanding, but to the medievalism of the imagination, which often identifies itself with a dream territory. In England, this is emphasized by the destruction of so many of the monuments of the middle ages after the Tudor settlement, so that in the eighteenth century a medieval interest is often synonymous with an interest in ruins.

In England, 'romantic' gradually approached literature through its application to scenes and buildings. Addison, in his *Remarks on Several Parts of Italy* in 1705, writes: 'We were here shown at a distance the Desarts that have been render'd so famous by the Penance of *Mary*

[1] *Die romantische Schule*, 1836.

Magdalene, who, after her Arrival with *Lazarus* and *Joseph of Arithmathea at Marseilles*, is said to have wept away the rest of her life among these solitary Rocks and Mountains. It is so Romantic a Scene, that it has always probably given occasion to such Chimerical Relations.' Gray seems somewhat to extend the meaning in his description in 1739 of the Grande Chartreuse: 'one of the most solemn, the most romantic, and the most astonishing scenes I ever beheld.' The entrance of the term into critical vocabulary is blocked by the word 'gothic'. The elements in architecture, literary form, theme, and sensibility, which to the eighteenth century seemed medieval, fantastic, irregular or wild, were 'gothic'. Shaftesbury in his *Characteristics* (1711) employed the word in its meaning of 'medieval' when he wrote that the Elizabethan dramatists were 'the first of Europeans who since the Gothick *Model* of Poetry, attempted to throw off the horrid Discord of jingling Rhyme'. Further 'gothic' was opposed to classical: Hurd in his *Letters on Chivalry and Romance* speaks of the *Faerie Queene* as a 'Gothic not classical poem'. When 'romantic' became a literary term and succeeded 'gothic' it gathered around the central conception of medieval the more general suggestion of fantastic and far-fetched which it had possessed in its earliest employment.

The term 'romantic', originating in England, was given a wider currency from its employment by Rousseau. From France it went to Germany to be built up more precisely into a literary expression. Eckermann in *Gespräche mit Goethe* reports Goethe as claiming the dubious honour of introducing the term into Germany. In the conversation for 21 March,

1830, Goethe has been speaking of the composition of his Walpurgis night: 'I have, however, endeavoured to mark out everything in distinct outline, in the antique style, so that there may be nothing vague or undecided, which might suit the romantic style well enough. The idea of the distinction between classical and romantic poetry, which is now spread over the whole world, and occasions so many quarrels and divisions, came originally from Schiller and myself. I laid down the maxim of objective treatment in poetry and would follow no other; but Schiller, who worked quite in the subjective way, deemed his fashion the right one.... The Schlegels took up this idea, so that it has now been diffused over the whole world; and everyone talks about classicism and romanticism—of which nobody thought fifty years ago.' From Germany the expression came back to France through Madame de Staël, who, in her *De l'Allemagne*, was assisted by Schlegel. V. Hugo in his preface to *Nouvelles Odes*[1] says that she was the first to use the expression 'litterature romantique' in France. From this continental tour, 'romantic' returns to England with its meaning modified. It is in reference to the French and German discussions that Byron uses the term in his reply to William Lisle Bowles in 1821: 'Schlegel and Madame de Staël have endeavoured to reduce poetry to *two* systems, classical and romantic. The effect is only beginning.' Byron, it has been suggested,[2] had been reading Stendhal's *Racine et Shakespeare*.

The history of the English share in this term 'romantic'

[1] Quoted, Logan Pearsall Smith, loc. cit.
[2] W. P. Ker in 'The Humanist Ideal': *Collected Essays*, Vol. II, 1925.

is typical of the history of romanticism in England. The term originated with us, and much of our eighteenth century lay behind the newer movements in France and Germany. In England, the terms lacked precision, never becoming the weapon of a school or movement, and in the same way the work associated by criticism with the term was with few exceptions not developed aggressively but in relation to other and earlier traditions. Thomas Warton in describing Dante[1] as 'this wonderful compound of classical and romantic fancy' had anticipated Goethe's use, but English critics and artists seemed to find no necessity to develop the term. Nor in England have we felt any necessity of reaching that precise definition of the 'romantic' at which the French precision of Brunetière aimed. Nor has English criticism evolved the elaborate scaffolding of a theory around 'romanticism' which the Germans have attempted. With them, theory is pursued for its own sake apart from the examples it illustrates. This can be seen culminating in work such as that of Fritz Strich.[2] For him classicism is man's desire for completion, and romanticism his longing for a perfection never to be fully attained. In contrast, the term grows up in England almost unnoticed and gradually becomes grafted on to literature. The need for it was there before it appeared, as can be seen by the earlier use of the partly synonymous terms, 'liberty', 'fancy', 'gothic', 'picturesque', and sometimes even that ambiguous term 'nature' in some of its earlier meanings. Nor is this contrast with French and German practice accidental,

[1] *History of English Poetry*, Vol. III, 1781, p. 241.
[2] *Deutsche Klassik und Romantik*, Munich, 1922.

for in England 'romantic' and 'classical' had existed in a degree of compromise not found elsewhere but typical of our national talent.

The expression 'Romantic Revolt', as applied to certain aspects of early nineteenth-century poetry, was not a contemporary expression. The poets of that period did not call themselves 'romantic', nor with the exception of Byron do they employ the word in the criticism of poetry. Wordsworth thinks of 'romantic' in its early eighteenth-century sense of something extravagant and excessive, even undesirable. Writing in 1808 to Coleridge on a collection which is being raised for some orphans he comments that too large a sum would raise 'much irregular and romantic expectation in distressed persons'. In his verse he uses 'romance' for a story of improbable adventure as in Spenser or the *Arabian Nights*. On the few occasions that he employs the adjective 'romantic' it is in the same sense. On one occasion in *The Prelude* he applies the term, still in the eighteenth-century sense, to scenery, 'renowned for beauty':

> That streamlet whose blue current works its way
> Between romantic Dovedale's spiry rocks.[1]

Even here the word does not occur in the earlier version of the passage. Wordsworth did not describe his own poetry as 'romantic'. Probably he would have been more prepared to consider his own work as a reaction against the 'romantic' in any sense in which he understood the word. Apart from the single instance quoted from *The Prelude* he finds no necessity for using it in

[1] *The Prelude*, VI, pp. 193-4.

Gray's sense of 'picturesque', partly because he had so little need to discuss the 'picturesque' at all.

The same is true of Shelley, who in the whole of his verse uses the expression 'romance' only once, in *Epipsychydion*:

> O antique verse and high romance.

His only employment of 'romantic' is in *Peter Bell, The Third*:

> To see what was romantic there.

The expression 'Romantic Movement' belongs, in England, to later nineteenth-century criticism, and it is with justice that W. P. Ker complained that the Romantic Revival, 'a convenient label in histories, is treated as if it were a scientific explanation'.[1]

The value of the term during the so-called 'Romantic Revival' is best illustrated by John Foster's essay, *On the Application of the Epithet Romantic*, first published in 1805. Foster, who revised his essay up to 1823, had no conception that it could be applied to contemporary literature, though he was a friend of Coleridge and his group. He uses it, as Wordsworth had done, in relation to one type of fiction, or in the early eighteenth-century sense of something opposed to fact. 'For having partly quitted the rank of plain epithets', Foster writes, 'it has become a convenient exploding word, of more special deriding significance than the other words of its order, such as wild, extravagant, visionary.' Almost in the manner of Bacon or Hobbes he writes that the authors of romances have yielded to 'the ascendancy of imagination over judgment. . . . They could drive on their career

---

[1] 'The Humanist Ideal', in *Collected Essays*, Vol. II, 1925.

through monstrous absurdities of description and narration without being sensible of inconsistency and improbability and with an air as if they really reckoned on being believed'. He suggested that the romances were 'a kind of mental balloon, far mounting into the air from the ground of ordinary experience'. He saw a danger in these extravagances, and in the extremes of sensibility which they may induce: 'the whole mind may become at length something like a hemisphere of cloud-scenery.' While his central thought still concentrates on the romances he seems to make a gesture of condemnation to the Rousseauist visionary. The romantic mind, he suggests, 'is content with ignorance, because environed with something more delicious than such knowledge, in the Paradise which imagination creates'. Foster's essay, valuable in itself, has the additional significance that neither he nor his contemporaries thought it applicable to the poetry and the criticism which later writers have described as 'romantic'. To attempt to reduce all the varied accomplishment of the early nineteenth century into a single generalization is to lose truth in the false simplicity of a formula.

While the term 'romantic' has endured many sea-changes, 'classical' has maintained a steadier meaning. In its simplest form 'classical' has been used to signify the imitation of the style and manner of Greek and Latin literature, or more precisely certain aspects of those literatures, for numerous critics have indicated that often the ancient authors depart from the principles ordinarily associated with their art. 'Classical' has not been confined to this meaning for it has been applied to pictorial art, to music, and like 'romantic' it has been used to describe a quality. J. C. Fillmore, writing of music,[1] has given a comprehensive definition to which most of the others can be referred. 'In classical music', he writes, 'form is first and emotional content subordinate; in romantic music content is first and form subordinate. The classical ideal is predominantly an intellectual one. Its products are characterized by clearness of thought, by completeness and symmetry, by harmonious proportion, by simplicity and repose. Classical works, whether musical or literary, are positive, clear, finished.' Goethe was reaching out in the same direction when he wrote that: 'romanticism is disease: classicism is health: the point is for the work to be thoroughly good, then it is sure to be classical.'

No useful conception of 'classical' in English literature can be found in the limited definition of the imitation of Greek and Latin literature. The direct influence of Greek literature on English has been surprisingly small. Chapman, though he translated Homer, wrote like a barbarian, whose great, tough, genius involved itself in complexities far removed from any possible conception of a Greek ideal. Ben Jonson, despite his acquaintance with Greek, is Latin in his origins when those origins are not English. Shelley, who studied Greek closely and used Greek mythology for his most effective expression in *Prometheus Unbound*, has obviously departed completely from any adherence to Greek motives or values. Tennyson, Browning, Swinburne and Landor, though they study Greek, employ that knowledge in verse to which classical principles have made only a minor contribution. Milton stands apart and to Milton I return.

When classical literature does enter into English to

A History of Pianoforte Music, 1885.

affect imaginative work it comes with few exceptions from Latin origins, or from translations of Latin work, or from French and Italian interpretations of classical literature. Latin influences, and in tragedy the not very reputable one of Seneca, are behind Elizabethan drama. These are known even to those who, like Shakespeare and Polonius, found 'Plautus too light and Seneca too heavy'. Dryden, who loved the classics as much perhaps as any English writer, was far happier with Latin than with Greek. He used Latin versions of Homer and Theocritus, and 'Longinus' he knew through Boileau and John Hall.[1] Latin influences are again behind the eighteenth century, with Horace mainly in Pope, and Juvenal in Johnson.

Those who followed Latin literature lived within a tradition, and here one approaches the distinction between 'classical' and 'romantic' which has the widest recognition and the most general utility. 'Classical' comes to mean most broadly a literature that recognizes a tradition, even if that tradition is not based precisely on classical literature, and 'romantic' signifies 'individual', even 'revolutionary'. The contrast has its reflection in literary criticism with the substitution of 'creation' for 'imitation' as a description of the way in which literature is made. It is the distinction emphasized by Coleridge between 'the objective poetry of the ancients and the subjective mood of the moderns': the contrast which leads Pope to find poetry in commonplace material exquisitely expressed, and Wordsworth to insist that poetry begins with the individual experience. Much of the emphasis of the distinction is on formal aspects, the elements defined by Aristotle, which Italian

[1] Mark van Doren, *The Poetry of Dryden*, 1920.

Renaissance criticism with considerable misrepresentation converted into a series of dogmas. Shakespeare, who wrote in an age of critical discussion, without himself writing literary criticism apart from the asides in the plays, summarized the distinction in Polonius's comment of 'the law of writ and the liberty' in drama. 'The law of writ', considered in its application to verse and drama, had its own complications, for Latin literature often derives, not always with full comprehension, from the Greek, with an elevation of certain patterns in composition. For writers in England, from the sixteenth century to the eighteenth, the purpose of following a classical ideal is entangled with the canonization of certain forms of Renaissance criticism.

The distinction in form is not confined to the technical aspects of poetry: it carries over into the theme the sentiment and the treatment. Whatever may be true in Greek or Latin literature itself, the writer of a classical adherence seeks a theme that has a central reference to human experience, often to normal human experience. Pope defined this ideal clearly when following Horace through Boileau he defined poetry as:

> What oft was thought but ne'er so well expressed.

The definition, though in a different context, was used by Ben Jonson to describe the method of his 'humours' comedies. Jonson is thinking of the contrast between his plays and the comedies of Shakespeare, to which later criticism has attached the name 'romantic'. Jonson studies manners, and retains throughout in his portrayal of the individual a strong social reference. Shakespeare explores emotions which, from a commonsense point of view, are elaborate, excessive and extravagant. The sentiment which Shakespeare pictures derives, with many modifications, through Spenser and Chaucer, from the French romances. Within that tradition and all its amplifications to Tennyson there lies the most permanent and distinctive conception of conduct which is away from the normal. It was from the realization of this distinction between normality and the later romances of the seventeenth century that the term 'romantic', as has been seen, first gained currency.

The distinction, at first applied to sentiment, extends to other forms of conduct distinct from the normal, and to the revolt of the individual against institutions or the domination of the intellect. Even here English literature develops in an individual way. In France the revolt of the individual works out aggressively in the philosophy of Rousseau. While there are few references of a precisely literary nature in Rousseau, his whole thought is in opposition to the pseudo-classical standards of which Boileau had been the greatest exponent in criticism, and of which Voltaire was the great eighteenth-century champion. Beyond this, his appeal, in as far as it was philosophical, was against the empiricism of Locke which had gained an international reputation. Under Locke's influence the imagination was discredited, while with Rousseau it is reasserted exultantly. Instead of the sober light of judgment there is a desire for a day-dream world, *un pays des chimères*. The whole structure is anti-intellectual, primitive, revolutionary. Incidentally it may be noted that Rousseau had no enduring influence on English literature. Coleridge and Wordsworth are for a time affected by his teaching, but they see through it. Shelley alone succumbs under Godwin's adaptations from Rousseau, but even with him the influence is not permanent. The emphasis given by Rousseau to individual experience leads, as Mario Praz has shown, to that quest in the nineteenth century for new and strange sensibilities without the restriction of any moral or social restraint, in the belief that the accompanying sense of power may induce new sensations. Such an attitude accompanied by genius can be found in Rimbaud. This unrestricted independence of the artist is well described by E. A. Poe: 'Imagination, feeling herself for once unshackled, roamed at will among the ever-changing wonders of a shadowy and unstable land.'[1] It is difficult to find any English poet of the first order who speaks in that way of his work.

Whether the terms 'classical' or 'romantic' be found convenient or not, it is clear that there is a contrast between work which is limited, direct, traditional, humble even, and work which is illimitable, aggressive, proud. As T. E. Hulme has suggested, the latter will be found most frequently allied to a revolutionary philosophy which emphasizes development and progress and holds to a Faustian conception of man's possibilities. The former will emerge from a distrust of the individual, and a consciousness of the necessary check of tradition, morality, and religion upon his vanities and his potentiality for evil. This contrast will be maintained when any narrower distinction between 'classical' and a rebellion from the 'classical' has broken down. As has already been suggested, these contrasts work out in England in a manner different from that of other Western European countries, and without extremes. There is in English

[1] *Adventure of one Hans Pfaal*: quoted by Irving Babbitt, in *Rousseau and Romanticism*, 1919.

verse a greater continuity, with the intrusion over centuries of elements to which the term 'romantic' may be applied, but seldom without other elements drawn from the past intermingled. From this sense of interdependence, along with tolerance in criticism, has emerged what is distinctive and characteristic in our poetry. My aim has been to explore that tradition, and it would appear that a beginning can be made with Chaucer. The issue can be conceived in a different way in Anglo-Saxon poetry, but with Chaucer a new start is made.

III

CHAUCER TO SHAKESPEARE

AS a narrative poet Chaucer had before him at least three possible opportunities: the English alliterative verse, the courtly poetry of the French romances and the *Roman de la Rose*, and Boccaccio's new, ambitious narrative, which attempted under early Renaissance influence to elevate narrative into epic. In lyric, he had the native tradition and the French and Italian forms. His choice is of great significance for the later history of our poetry. His education and social environment prevented him from accepting the native tradition: alliterative verse was 'rym ram ruf by lettre', and the native lyric and the ballad obviously attracted him less than the elaborate French forms of the rondeau and ballade. So dominant was their appeal that even the sonnet, which he knew, he did not practise. The one limitation in Chaucer's vision is his disdain, for it seems no less, of the popular and native traditions. While he gave so much else to poetry, he stunted the native forms at a time when they might have been transformed with the aid of his genius.

Apart from this rejection Chaucer's outlook seems one of happy open-mindedness. To exploit one form, he does not reject others. He brings into his conceptions of poetry, and into the criticism which his experiments imply, a sense of compromise, of the union of opposites, which has been one of the most distinguishing and characteristic features of our poetry. He is aware of the courtly French romances and the elaborate traditions of *amour courtois* which they employed. He may feel that they have existed too long, and are too antiquated for imitation, but it is almost with longing that he looks back on them. They had flourished for two centuries, and to the ruling classes, to those who read French, they had long been familiar. In England, the vernacular imitations of them had clung to some resemblance of the story while losing the sentiment, and thus missed the main purpose for which the originals had been contrived. These English romances gained from Chaucer only the satire of *Sir Thopas*, but his genuine attachment to the involved sentiment behind the romances can be seen in his confession of an affection for the *Roman de la Rose*. The French romances had been killed by the *Roman de la Rose* apart from anything that happened in England. As W. P. Ker writes: 'it extracted the quintessence of the old romantic poetry, the amatory sentiment which had always been the chief interest of the French romances. When once this had been disengaged from the story of adventures, and turned into allegory, it was impossible to put it back into its old body.'[1] England was discovering this most distinctively medieval way in poetry when the middle ages were over, and much of the later verse which has been called 'romantic' is an attempt to make good that loss. Chaucer more than once looked back wistfully at themes, possible for treatment in the manner of the romances, but concluded that they were too old to be

[1] *Form and Style in Poetry*, 1928.

rehandled. The Wife of Bath lived in a common-sense world that looked upon the romances as a dream of far-off forgotten things.

> In tholde dayes of the kyng Arthour,
> Of which that Britons speken greet honour,
> All was this land fulfild of fayerye.
> The elf-queen, with hir Joly companye,
> Daunced ful ofte in many a grene mede;
> This was the olde opinion as I rede,
> I speke of manye hundred yeres ago.

In the *Squire's Tale*, when Chaucer approaches that 'courtesie' which was at the centre of the tradition of sentiment in the romances, it is with the same gentleness:

> With so heigh reverence and obeisaunce
> As wel in speche as in countenance,
> That Gawain with his olde curteisye,
> Though he were come ageyn out of Fairye,
> Ne coude him not amende with a word.

He had in Boccaccio a model in narrative offering greater possibilities than the old tradition, and in *Troilus and Criseyde* he went beyond Boccaccio, discovering for himself a way of translating the whole of what he saw in life around him into poetry. Realism may be the best name for what he achieved in parts of that poem, though it is a clumsy word. He gained the effect, not to be found again until Shakespeare in the mature tragedies, of a world around the story. While so much in *Troilus and Criseyde* is original and independent he had selected a theme well known and often exploited. He had chosen, as J. L. Lowes comments, like most great artists, not an invented theme but one which had 'come down to him through centuries, growing and deepening in content and import as it came, and shifting, chameleon-like, its colour with its period and its narrators'.[1]

His success in *Troilus and Criseyde* might well have 'disteyned' for him the older tradition of the romances with the elegances and the gentle extravagance of sentiment. If English poetry had been constructed by minds who thought in the harsh and discordant terms of 'schools' of poetry and of 'movements' it might well have been so. For Chaucer, the victory over a new territory of the imagination left what was past still lively in its own colours, and desirable even if no longer to be achieved. The proof of this lies in the *Prologue* to *The Legend of Good Women*, in his return to allegory, to the Garden of the Rose, to the dream-vision of the God of Love, to the unmatchable ballade of Absolon and to his confession of his defections from his 'devocioun' to the sentiment of the romances. He had gained the knowledge that experience can be explored at different levels of sensibility. The philosophy of Boethius, the bawdries of the tales of the Shipman and the Miller, the moralizing of Melibeus, the romantic tradition of the French courtly poetry, and the reality of *Troilus and Criseyde* were all held within his mind. The stain of mortality which later affects both Shakespeare and Donne seldom conflicts with his enjoyment, and he accepts the distresses of life without apparent anger: 'but for the shynyng of thy forme', he writes in his translation of Boethius, 'that is to seyn, the beautee of thy body, how swiftly passinge is it, and how transitorie; certes, it is more flittinge than the mutabilitee of flowers of the somer-sesoun.' The knowledge of 'mutabilitee' was there but the 'somer-sesoun' no less enjoyed: it does not

[1] *Geoffrey Chaucer*, 1934.

corrupt the mood of the *Prologue* to *The Legend of Good Women*. Had Chaucer acted differently, and rejected the sentiment of the romances, the whole course of our literature might have been different. His equability, and his power of exploring more than one way in verse are more responsible than any other influence, Shakespeare's alone apart, for developing that happy mingling of forms which is the distinctive feature of our English tradition. The consequence was that in England the medieval matter and the medieval romantic sentiment lived on and flourished in the sixteenth century, despite the new learning and the Renaissance. With modifications they can still be found in the nineteenth century in Tennyson and Meredith.

His way in poetry could not be repeated, but it left its strong influence on the tradition. It could not be repeated, for apart from the false distinctions of 'schools' and 'movements' there remains the inevitable change that comes in literature with the modification of the human mind itself, and the world that it perceives. In Chaucer's world each thing was in its place, heaven, hell, God, the sun, the planets, the Evil One, and the societies of men. They have all changed their places since, or disappeared, and many minds have sought to find in some unique experience a refashioning of the broken fragments of what now seems a vision but was then the reality. The increasing self-consciousness and inwardness of thought, apart from all other considerations, separate Chaucer from the seventeenth century, just as his pathos and sentiment separate him from the heroic age of *Beowulf* or *Maldon*. This will not prevent a poet in any age from going back to Chaucer's way. He cannot go back completely, for the bottom of Chaucer's world has fallen out. If he goes back in servile imitation he can add nothing to the enrichment of poetry. But in a different way, he may employ something for some urgent and fresh purpose of his own, and so lead to the development of poetry. Such a development has of course no necessary connexion with any theory of progress.

Chaucer's success serves unfortunately to minimize Langland's achievement. That Spenser knew Langland is obvious, but Chaucer and Chaucer's models influence him more potently. Langland disappears as an active influence in English poetry from the time of Spenser to his uncertain reintroduction in the nineteenth century. His name is known to critics, and a few may know of the poem behind the name, but no great poet subjects himself to his influence. Langland had everything against him, a language more remote than Chaucer's, and a verse form that from the sixteenth century had little support. Yet the purposes towards which some later poets struggled Langland achieved. In *Piers Plowman* he achieved the Christian poem which in the seventeenth century occupied so many stout minds, including Dryden's. He gave the portrait of contemporary society and manners, and their spiritual background, which Coleridge urged upon Wordsworth as the proper subject for a long poem. Like Spenser he wished to serve God and his country, which to him could be achieved in one and the same way, by the *salus animarum*. In his own age his verse must have gone abroad to a wider audience[1] than that of Chaucer, for in his frequent use of the vernacular sermon as Dr. Owst has shown[2] he was the poetical interpreter of a wide

[1] The audience of Chaucer and Langland is a theme still unexplored.
[2] *Literature and Pulpit in Medieval England*, p. 549, 1933.

audience: 'the *Vision of Piers Plowman*', Dr. Owst writes, 'represents nothing more or less than the quintessence of English medieval preaching gathered up in a single metrical piece of unusual charm and vivacity.' Langland is the nearest approach to Dante in English poetry. English verse lacks a *Divina Commedia*, but *Piers Plowman* is our closest approach to the *Purgatorio*. Had Langland come through, with whatever modification, as a great Christian and mystical poet into the sixteenth century, the tradition of our poetry would have been enriched. While there is this failure in Chaucer to concede a place to a powerful native tradition, his attitude in other ways was open-minded and the importance of the resulting compromise can be seen in the sixteenth century when Spenser in the *Faerie Queene* breaks through with a new poetry.

The direct influence in verbal recollections or the choice of identical themes may be slight, but it was Chaucer's example which, with the help of the Italians, opened up the road for Spenser. The individually English compromise between extremes illustrates itself in a distinctive way in his work. No poet in England, with the sole exception of Milton, gave more thought to the production of a poetry that was classical. Few poets have produced work whose effect and influence have been less classical. His earliest ambitions, led by Gabriel Harvey, were towards 'imitation' in its narrowest sense, the reproduction in English of classical hexameters. His good sense and his awareness of the pattern of the Italian romances led him to avoid that futility. Form remained the major preoccupation of his mind, and form that should emulate the classical conception of the epic. As his preface to Sir Walter Raleigh shows, he intended his poem to be 'a poem historical', that is an epic in the Homeric and Vergilian manner, with an influence too from Ariosto and Tasso, whom he regarded as within the same tradition. Yet whatever may be his preconceptions about form, in his actual performance everything is changed. He has added allegory. This may come superficially through the Italian theorists or from Tasso, but fundamentally it is his contact with the strongest and most unyielding medieval tradition. Thus the poet who is attempting in the motives of his work to be Tudor, Protestant, and anti-Catholic retains contact with the oldest and most abused medieval convention. Ariosto, despite all his elaborations, has a plan in his poem. Spenser's plan is all in the preface. The poem reveals no design and remains unfinished. The poet who set out to imitate a classical ideal ended by creating a world of 'mental space'.

One of his critics, Janet Spens, in her discriminating study,[1] has been led to believe that he conceived the poem in a popular form on the theme of the Seven Deadly Sins and that this he remodelled at Raleigh's instigation, hastily and immediately before the first publication. The inconsistencies which Janet Spens finds in the poem, are there, though not so many as she would suggest,[2] but to explain them not as a natural sequence of Spenser's diffuseness but as a hasty revision is, I think, to misunderstand his mind, and indeed to set too hard a rule upon the workings of the poetic mind in general. The poet who conceived the intricacy of

---

[1] *Spenser's Faerie Queene*, 1934.

[2] She finds an inconsistency between the 'Bower of Bliss' and 'The Gardens of Adonis' but see C. S. Lewis on this in *The Allegory of Love*, 1936.

pattern of *The Shepheardes Calendar* is not the poet to revert to a simple popular method of story-telling, while the explicit promise of an ambitious poem in the epic manner is to be found in the October eclogue. The explanation lies rather in the conflict between two loyalties: his intellect is dominated by interests in theory and abstract form, by the classical, but his genius as a poet leads him into other ways, far removed. It is true that he is more sympathetic to native verse than Chaucer had been, and his sympathy is one of the motives for his experiments in diction, especially in *The Shepheardes Calendar*, where the alliteration shows that *Piers Plowman* was more to him than a name. Had Chaucer discovered some way of combining native elements with the courtly tradition, Spenser's poetry and much else in English poetry might have been different. As it is, though Spenser clearly sees beyond the court, it is from within the court that he looks out at the world.

In other ways Spenser is more removed from reality than Chaucer, especially the Chaucer of *Troilus and Criseyde*. He retains the world of chivalry, which Thomas Warton described as 'revenging injuries, and doing justice to the distressed: which was the proper business and ultimate end of knight-errantry'. Spenser could use such motives, for in Elizabethan England, in the 'nineties of the sixteenth century, chivalry had become topical, fashionable, and courtly. The methods of the ages of chivalry, long dead as far as realistic warfare was concerned, lived on in the decorative life of Elizabeth's court, in the pageants designed to entertain the Queen, and in the tilt-yards where Gloriana watched Essex and her other nobles perform. The Lady of the Lake had been one of the pageants at Kenilworth, and in Spenser's own April eclogue he names the nymphs who gather round Eliza as 'Ladyes of the lake'. Even outside the court the practice of archery was conducted by 'the friendly and frank fellowship of prince *Arthur's knightes* in and about the citie of London'.[1]

It is true, as C. S. Lewis suggests,[2] that 'beneath the surface of Spenser's poem is the world of popular imagination; almost, a popular mythology; but it is well below the surface. What was clearly and continually visible was the world of chivalry, and it is difficult to know just how far that world was removed from the minds of his contemporaries. Clearly he was not constructing, as some later poets have done, a world adapted to his own sensibility to which he could escape from contemporary life. He is sharing in that Elizabethan power of attaching poetry to magnificence, releasing it from the ephemeral and the foulness with which the ordinary, everyday life was surrounded. He seemed, like some others of his contemporaries, able to gather up the pageantry of medieval chivalry and keep it as a ceremonial, and at no period does poetry walk more comfortably with these emblazonments.

At the same time, he retained a strong moral and social reference, with a clear conception of the function of the poet in relation to society. He wished under God and his Queen to elevate his own country, its language, and its ways of life. Modern criticism, particularly with W. L. Renwick[3] and C. S. Lewis,[4] has recaptured with clarity this aspect of his art and shown that his vision saw a

[1] C. B. Millican in *The Review of English Studies*, VI, 22, 1930.
[2] *The Allegory of Love*, 1936.
[3] *Edmund Spenser*, 1925.
[4] *The Allegory of Love*, 1936.

court giving service under the Moral Virtues to the common people and *Piers Plowman* may have contributed to this aspect of his thought. Attractive though these elements in Spenser may be, artists who knew him best from his own age to this have been attracted by the ceremonial of the poem rather than by its ultimate moral and social purposes. For them he had retreated into a fairyland. So out of the compromise with different elements ever present in Spenser's poetry, the decorative, multi-coloured vision removed from reality remains dominant.[1] Here is the material to which the name 'romantic' can be given by any definition of the word. The typically English conclusion is that it has resulted from a poet whose purposes, as he prefigured them, were moral and classical.

We must in poetry accept what we are given, and Spenser gives abundantly; at the same time it may not be idle to speculate that the fortunes of our non-dramatic poetry might have been firmer if Spenser had discovered some form closer to reality and more intelligible as a whole to the ages that followed. Compared with Chaucer and with Shakespeare, his figures are removed from life. He had, of course, references to life through the moral allegory, and the historical allegory was topical, but nowhere was there great action worked out through living persons. Had he achieved that element of the epic, our non-dramatic poetry might have been secured on that same wide and enduring basis as the drama achieved with Shakespeare. As Janet Spens has shown[2], his method of allegory was far more natural

---

[1] He has also the grotesque, but this is not so well remembered by his more successful followers.

[2] *Spenser's Faerie Queene*, 1934.

and congenial to the Elizabethan age than later students have been prepared to credit: 'Spenser is essentially an Elizabethan, and the Elizabethans tended to utter their more intense emotions through the imagery of human figures.' But Chaucer came through that tradition, despite all his attachments to allegory, and so did Shakespeare. Had Spenser succeeded similarly, our poetry would have been richer than it is. The contrast can be seen most clearly by comparing his verse with the most human passages in Chaucer's *Troilus and Criseyde*, or with Shakespeare in the tragedies. These give the universals of human life in a form perpetually enduring while Spenser does not. He was assisting, against his own conscious purposes, in the very gradual process which would shift poetry from the centre of human thought, as an arbitrator of knowledge and conduct, to a dependence on the sensibilities over which reason could exercise no judgment. It is again distinctive of the English tradition that this conclusion was reached not by any aggressive assertion of critical theory but by a compromise with different traditions, and, in this instance, against the will of the poet himself.

There was one in Elizabeth's court who could enjoy Spenser's phantasy with a calculating eye. What did Francis Bacon think of Edmund Spenser and the fashions of courtly chivalry? He, too, believed in the ceremonial of life with beauty as its medium, but he would not permit the ceremonial or the beauty to interfere with the sober engagements of the mind, which were philosophy and science. It may have been his contemplation of Spenser's attempt to serve morality and society through an allegorical poem that led him to set down the absolute distinction which he came to discover between the purposes of science and poetry. For him beauty was tangible, an ornament of existence: 'the glimpses and beams of diamonds that strike the eye; Indian feathers that have glorious colours; the coming into a fair garden; the coming into a fair room richly furnished; a beautiful person, and the like.'[1] The term 'imagination' which came later to hold such a high place is frequently found in his work but always in the sense of something opposed to reason, fantastic, and even dangerous. So Pythagoras's conception 'that the world was one entire perfect living creature' is described as a 'monstrous imagination'. Witches, he reported, were imaginative for they 'believe oft-times they do that which they do not'. In more formal definition he discovered 'imagination' to be of three kinds: 'the first joined with the belief of that which is to come; the second joined with memory of that which is past; and the third of things present, or as if they were present; for I comprehend in this, imaginations feigned, and at pleasure: as if one should imagine such a man to be in the vestments of a pope or to have wings.'[2]

The application of such a conception of imagination to literature could only tend to effect the removal of poetry to some fairyland. Against the pride which the Renaissance had felt in the arts comes the voice of science asserting that 'the imagination; which being not tied to the laws of matter, may at pleasure join that which nature hath severed, and sever that which nature hath joined, and so make unlawful matches and divorces of things.... The use of this feigned history hath been to give some shadow of satisfaction to the mind of man

[1] *Natural History*, Cent. IX, 873.
[2] *Natural History*, Cent. X, 900.

in those points wherein the nature of things doth deny it'.[1] Poetry is set against reason and described as a snare, a sedative, and a pretentious delusion: 'therefore it was ever thought to have some participation of divineness, because it doth raise and erect the mind, by submitting the shews of things to the desires of the mind; whereas reason doth buckle and bow the mind unto the nature of things. And we see that by these insinuations and congruities with man's nature and pleasure, joined also with the agreement and consort it hath with music, it hath had access and estimation in rude times and barbarous regions, where other learning stood excluded.'

The moralists had often attacked poetry but that attack, as Sidney had shown, could be fenced off. Here was a more serious relegation of the arts to the periphery of life. The debate which Bacon aroused has been unending, for it is more fundamental than any issue of 'romantic' and 'classical'. It represents the gradual encroachment of a mechanical conception of the world upon all man's capacity for myth-making. The elements which were later defined as romantic are in Bacon found to be present in literature as a whole. Poetry was placed in a position of defence, but the awareness of the issue had come not from a poet or from one who was primarily a critic of poetry, but from a scientist and philosopher. Gradually the pressure of this criticism increased, and the poet, though not always consciously, found himself in a world inimical to his purposes. It is typical of Bacon's attitude that in *De Sapientia Veterum* he attempted to show that the wisdom of the ancients was contained allegorically in their myths. This may at first sight seem merely a return to the earlier methods

[1] *The Advancement of Learning*, Bk. II.

of the mythographers.[1] Actually it is the exercise of his rationalizing mind upon material whose imaginative power he distrusted, and often despised. The fundamental distinction which Bacon had stated so clearly, continues into the later seventeenth century: with Locke and with Bacon's followers in the Royal Society it is restated with an increased emphasis. Science is the progressive approach to the interpretation of phenomena through experiment and reasoning, while poetry is only a play among the shadows, the fables and the mythologies, heathen, grotesque and condemned. Spenser's world cannot be recreated once Bacon's world is generally accepted and understood. Even those who oppose Bacon's world become passively permeated with its values, and so poetry endures a change apart from any loyalties to schools of criticism. Here is the ultimate cause for the seventeenth-century attack on mythology which Milton alone resisted successfully. Our poetry might have stood against the attack more firmly had it had a mythology of its own, instead of a borrowed one. Science has continually increased the elements in life which it can explain. It may never undermine belief but it undermines the 'magical' world through which belief was once interpreted.

It is the great good fortune of our literature that Shakespeare had gone far in his career as a dramatist before the dilemma which Bacon indicated became apparent. The fortunate accident of his birth, coming when it did, allowed him to combine much from the middle ages, still fresh in the national memory, with the ambition in expression and the magnificence of the Renaissance.

[1] See *Mythology and the Renaissance Tradition*, Douglas Bush, Minneapolis, 1932.

His position had some parallels with that of Chaucer. He knew the tradition of the medieval romances and their courtly sentiments of love and he had, as Chaucer in *Troilus and Criseyde*, an awareness of the world around him, his own awareness. The medieval narratives did not themselves attract him. Even Chaucer, with a more limited choice at hand, had avoided them, but Shakespeare had Italian stories in plenty, and Holinshed, and North's translation of Plutarch. He accepted, as Chaucer had done, much of the sentiment of the courtly romances without accepting their themes, and he embedded that sentiment in diverse material in the plays to be known later as the 'romantic' comedies. Nor did the history plays and the tragedies escape contact with these medieval values in sentiment, though there the sentiment was not dominant. In his study of Spenser he had found the union of romantic sentiment with mariage and this he had accepted. The very idiom of the early 'romantic' comedies would have been impossible without the elements in the sentiment of the French courtly romances which Chaucer and Spenser had made English:

> O gentle Proteus; Love's a Mighty Lord,
> And hath so humbled me, as I confess
> There is no woe to his correction
> Nor to his service no such joy on earth.[1]

From the first, this presentation of romantic sentiment is challenged by a moral and intellectual vision of life. Even in *Love's Labour's Lost* he showed that his intelligence could see round this exaltation of sentiment, and in the midst of the early comedies he had written *Romeo*

[1] *The Two Gentlemen of Verona*, II, IV, 136.

and Juliet, showing what disaster its encouragement might effect. Yet whatever the intellect might suggest, he had been content in those early years to exploit the strange though limited world of beauty which romantic sentiment might suggest, with only such gentle concessions to reason as Bottom with an ass's head in *A Midsummer Night's Dream.* Gradually, either from some personal experience, or from some contact with contemporary circumstance or mode of thought, or possibly from the natural maturing of his art, he grew less patient with the phantasy and sometimes almost angry, as if he had been deceived. On the one hand the sighs, the vows, the gentleness, the adoration, and on the other passion, lechery, lust, and the traffic of the 'suburbs' with such a distress of spirit that the illusions of romantic sentiment seem something hateful:

> The expense of spirit in a waste of shame
> Is lust in action.

Before he disavowed romantic sentiment he had written *As You Like It* and *Twelfth Night.* Nothing approaching these could ever come into English drama again. They could only have been written at that period while the modern world was still close enough to the middle ages for the older courtesy to be remembered. The singularly fortunate circumstance is that they were written at the unique moment when their composition was possible.

Shakespeare's achievement renders meaningless in England the opposition of 'classical' and 'romantic' into completely opposing schools. He had developed the compromise which Chaucer had founded. The fairies, the witches, the haunted castles, and most of the later paraphernalia of romance are in the plays along with the romantic sentiment. In contrast there are the 'dark comedies' and Ulysses's speech on 'degree' and the austerity of the closing scenes of *Coriolanus*. If 'classical' be accounted the employment of traditional themes, Shakespeare had used the major figures of English history and of the ancient world, but on the other hand in *Macbeth* he had invented the romantic aggressor who sets himself against the moral order in an agony of self-torture. If 'romantic' be the exploration of unusual or abnomal sensibility it is here, but ever against the background and the values of a moral world. If 'classical' be the recording of traditional sentiments with clarity, his characters supply essays on charity, mercy, suicide and death, indeed a *vade mecum* of human experience. But again, his language in its imagery has that union of conscious and unconscious elements which seems later one of the most distinctive qualities of romantic diction. In a less obvious way he had broken with the classical conception of what poetic diction should be. He had so transformed the traditional language that it had become the medium of an unique experience.[1] Coleridge realized this when he wrote that Shakespeare's 'language is entirely his own.... The construction of Shakespeare's sentences, whether in verse or prose, is the necessary and homogeneous vehicle of his peculiar manner of thinking'.[2] His summary may be exaggerated, for much in Shakespeare's diction is necessarily 'common form', not easily distinguishable from his contemporaries, but what remains once this

[1] *The Jacobean Drama*, 1936, by U. M. Ellis-Fermor. Chap. XIII on Shakespeare's transmutation of language.
[2] *Table Talk*, March 15, 1834.

has been eliminated, shows a clear development of an increasingly elliptical expression of the 'before unapprehended relations of things'. To some writers in the eighteenth century, adhering to an ordered and traditional vocabulary, this proved a difficulty. Johnson in his *Preface* wrote that for Shakespeare a quibble was 'the fatal Cleopatra for which he lost the world, and was content to lose it'. At the same time Johnson, in commenting on Shakespeare's language in general, anticipates, as so often elsewhere, the findings of Coleridge. 'Shakespeare', he writes, 'is one of the original masters of our language.' Finally, in the more obvious aspects of literary form Shakespeare had from the first a freedom from any adherence to prescribed pattern, nor after Shakespeare could any unprejudiced mind dogmatize about the 'rules'. The freedom which he had claimed for himself he employed not with licence, but with its own law of developing invention to the uttermost bounds which his medium allowed. He never posturized in form or gave way to wilfulness or incoherence.

It is Shakespeare's practice, more than anything else, which separates the English discussion of 'classical' and 'romantic' from Continental values, though in his mingling of forms he is, as has been seen, only carrying on a national tradition, present in Chaucer and Spenser. The widespread and continuous interest in his work has, however, led English critics to employ his art as a criterion for testing general principles. No poet in England, no critic or dramatist of the first order, has failed to see that with Shakespeare the older distinctions have broken down. Pope, whose practice in art was so far removed from Shakespeare's, regarded him as of all English poets, 'the fairest and fullest subject for Criticism', and his art more directly in contact with 'Nature' than that of Homer. For Johnson, Shakespeare was already beginning 'to assume the dignity of an ancient'. Not only does Shakespeare break down the divisions of the 'schools' but he wins too easily, and undermines too liberally, the loyalties to order, and tradition, and the union of the intellect with poetry. The fault lies not with Shakespeare himself but with those who have praised him. The pity is that Coleridge and his contemporaries spoke so slightingly, and with such little knowledge, of eighteenth-century Shakespearian criticism. The danger is that from the eighteenth century onwards drama at its best was considered drama as Shakespeare wrote it, and that was inimitable. The tradition of Ben Jonson, valuable and contrasting, while strong in the early eighteenth century, suffers through the elevation of Shakespeare. Had Jonson come through as a living model into the nineteenth century he might have proved a more positive and useful pattern than Shakespeare for dramatists in an industrial age. Coleridge, it is true, realized that *The Alchemist* had the most perfect of plots, but he never explored Ben Jonson as he did Shakespeare.

Shakespeare, as interpreted in the nineteenth century, was the triumph of individual method and expression. The idolatry that surrounded him concealed from contemporary vision the virtues, modest but useful, of order and tradition. Even in the eighteenth century the romantic gains its victories too easily because the practice of Shakespeare renders every critic with classical loyalties uneasy about his own principles. At the same time because the victory is so easy, and because the romantic in England is ever compromised with other elements, the same extremes as are to be found in France and Germany are never reached. The most interesting document in proof is Johnson's *Preface to his Edition of Shakespear's Plays*, one of the bravest and most honest pieces of criticism ever written in our language. Yet in it Johnson, who in his survey of non-dramatic verse in his *Lives of the Poets*, stood firm for order and tradition, sold the pass too easily to romanticism. There are indications that he was himself perturbed by his boldness, though he had always the enjoyment of knowing that Voltaire was on the other side: 'Perhaps, what I have here not dogmatically but deliberately written, may recall the principles of the drama to a new examination. I am almost frighted at my own temerity: and when I estimate the fame and the strength of those that maintain the contrary opinion, am ready to sink down in reverential silence.' Did the critics of the later romantic periods avoid quoting from Johnson because they were ashamed to find how many of their findings were anticipated, or did his stricter judgments on non-dramatic poetry obscure for them the surrender of the *Preface to Shakespear's Plays*? As it was, Shakespearian idolatry in the early nineteenth century became in itself a bondage, as if the 'rules' had been reversed, and the new dogma established, less reasonable and less useful than the old. Evil counsels can be gained by distortions out of the writings of good men, equally from Aristotle and from Shakespeare.

IV

DONNE TO MILTON

THAT our literature was singularly fortunate not only in Shakespeare's genius but in the time of its appearance can be seen by contrasting his work with that of his contemporary, John Donne. The difference arises in part from studies, from temperament and genius, and other imponderables, but there remain certain elements arising out of the changed intellectual atmosphere in which Donne moved. Life is continually presenting some new awareness, either in material circumstances or in spiritual conceptions, which demands new adjustments. Some such change came with marked emphasis at the end of the sixteenth and the beginning of the seventeenth centuries. Science had encroached on belief, and of that encroachment Donne was profoundly aware. Once science had invited attention to its own anatomy of the world, the fables, mythologies, and even all the hierarchies of sentiments and images, which poets had used, seemed unacceptable and childish. The most obvious instance of the change is in Donne's dismissal of myth, for which Carew praised him. Other poets, Carew suggests,

> will recall the godly exiled train
> Of gods and goddesses, which in thy just reign
> Was banish'd nobler poems; and now with these

> Shall stuff their lines, and swell the windy page
> Till verse, refined by thee in this last age,
> Turn ballad-rhyme, or those old idols be
> Adored again with new apostacy.

The challenge that Bacon had set down was that poetry dealt only with a world of shadows, the imaginative kinsmen of superstitions. That is a challenge which Donne accepts. Consequently the orientation of his mind, and more generally the orientation which the scientific attitude had made inevitable, led to the banishment of many elements which contributed to a romantic tradition as it had developed up to that time. Part of that romantic world came back again, but with its colours changed. Spenser and the world of chivalry went out and never returned in the same way. Arthur and his knights are a perpetual theme, but only in the nineteenth century with Tennyson do they supply material for a major writer, and then only with a modified satisfaction. The loss of the Grecian mythology was far greater. The Grecian gods are not domesticated again in any English poem by a writer of the first magnitude until Keats composes the *Hyperion*. The major difficulty in the poetry of the seventeenth century and of the eighteenth is this absence of a mythology. The problem, as will appear later, gains ample critical formulation by Dryden. It is implicit in the poetry of Pope.

In his lyrics Donne attacked the poetic methods by which romantic sentiment had been presented. The abrupt impatience of his verse is his criticism of elaborate adornment, the tradition of Spenser and the Petrarchans. As a poet of love, he had passion, satire, and a rare and compressed beauty, but he could never bring himself to admire the intricate game of courtesy as it might be found from Chaucer onwards. If so much was dismissed, what remained? Donne in rejecting the adorned language of Spenser, the tradition which Dante had so well described of making the texture of poetry as spendid as possible, had the alternative at hand of making verse in a vocabulary possessing a terse, rapid movement that gave the appearance of a conversational idiom. He accompanied that experiment in vocabulary with satire, an attempt to strip man of the elegances with which the romantic tradition had surrounded him, and show him anatomized, with an emphasis on the unfriendly and disconcerting elements. The ghost of beauty walks still among his skulls and his cere-cloths, the bracelet of bright hair about the bone, the memory not wholly exorcized of the romantic beauty he has deliberately set aside.

In the twentieth century his reputation as a poet has been elevated. In part this is just and compensatory for long neglect. Yet he fell short of one aspect of greatness by the doubtful quality of his seriousness. His learning, medieval and contemporary, was used at times captiously as if he consoled himself for some incapacity to integrate his knowledge by playing with it in complicated patterns as he exploited his troubled passion. The mind had become self-conscious in Donne's poetry, separated from wisdom, and the poet himself had lost that conception of his relationship to society, and a purpose to fulfil. This quality of his mind and of his poetry lingers in the memory of the reader when Donne's religious poetry is approached. Without that background his religious poetry might be accepted as his solution for the dilemma of his mind and of his period. Probably it is, but the recollection of his use of the intellect as a destructive element lingers and affects our judgment.

When all allowance has been made, the ultimate and most vital expression of his thought is to be found in *An Anatomie of the World*, and *The Progresse of the Soule* and the *Anniversaries*. If the new science had closed some of the ways in which the world was to be interpreted, and even if the material world was in decay[1] 'ad senescentem mundum', the road to religion still remained open. He accepted that solution not with the half-heartedness of some nineteenth-century poets, not with the hesitations of *In Memoriam*, but with a sense of processional triumph that has disturbed some of his readers. Here, in one of the interpretations of the term, was his most romantic approach to poetry, but he was exulting over the 'march of intellect' and over the new science not as some nineteenth-century poets by the creation of a personal imaginative world, but by reasserting a faith, Catholic in essence, and based on St. Thomas Aquinas. Yet even in this triumph the memory of the anatomizing intellect remains, as a cicatrice upon the image created, and one realizes that something has changed, never perhaps to be wholly repaired.

The dilemma for which Donne found his solution appears in an instructive way in the work of Abraham Cowley. While Donne is the original and exploring genius, Cowley is the popularizer, precocious but never profound. The solution for Cowley was easy because he never thought deeply. He is sensitive of the changes in the mental atmosphere of his time, but he has neither the poetic skill nor the depth of experience to carry his

[1] See R. F. Jones, *Ancients and Moderns*, St. Louis, 1936.

own intentions into adequate performance. Nothing is more misleading in an estimate of his poetry than the importance attached to the often-quoted passage from his essay *Of Myself*. Here he writes of the volume of Spenser's works that lay in his mother's parlour: 'this I happened to fall upon, and was infinitely delighted with the Stories of the Knights, and Gyants and Monsters, and brave Houses, which I found everywhere there.' Whatever may have been the enthusiasms of his childhood, in manhood he became aware of the new science which unlike Donne he embraced with eagerness, if never with much knowledge or understanding. To his facile and resilient mind the compromise between science and poetry would be an easy one, though he never explains how it could come about. Of this he was certain, Spenser and the world of chivalry must go, and with them the world of Greek mythology. The myths might be used as the ornaments of poetry, but never as its informing basis. The attitude is not confined to Cowley, but as he was so absorbent of the atmosphere of his age, the change can be seen most clearly working in him. An attempt had been made to revive the vitality of myth through allegory as in Sandys's translation of the *Metamorphoses* in 1632, but in the later seventeenth century even this dubious stronghold was attacked.[1] Mythology driven out of the work of the greater artists continued an underworld existence in such volumes of popular instruction as Tooke's *Pantheon*.

Cowley in rejecting mythology retained religion as a poetic theme. He is guided possibly by Donne's example, for his religious poetry is never actuated by

[1] See Douglas Bush, *Mythology and the Renaissance Tradition*, 1932.

any personal or intimate motive. He assumes that Christian stories can be substituted for epic themes to replace the myths and the romances of chivalry which he has rejected. In *Davideis* he made the attempt and in the preface[1] he states his aim: 'those mad Stories of the *Gods* and *Heroes*, seem in themselves so ridiculous; yet they were then the *whole* Body (or rather *Chaos*) of the *Theologie* of those times. . . . There was no other *Religion*, and therefore *that* was better than *none at all*. But to us who have no need of them, to us who deride their *folly*, and are wearied with their *impertinencies*, they ought to appear no better Arguments for *Verse*, than those of their worthy *Successors*, the *Knights Errant*.' This rejection of 'fancy' and mythology was accompanied with an enthusiasm for the new science. In his ode *To the Royal Society* he writes of Philosophy, 'great & only Heir' of human knowledge:

> That his own bus'ness he might quite forget,
> They amus'd him with the sports of wanton Wit,
> With the Desserts of Poetry they fed him,
> Instead of solid meats t' increase his force.

The day when Authority 'stalk'd about', like 'some old Giant's more Gigantick Ghost', has passed for 'Bacon has broke that Scare-crow Deitie':

> Behold the rip'ned Fruit come, gather now your Fill.
>   Yet still, methinks, we fain would be
>   Catching at the Forbidden Tree,
>   We would be like the Deitie,
> When Truth and Falsehood, Good and Evil, we
> Without the Senses aid within ourselves would see,
>   For 'tis God only who can find
>   All Nature in his Mind.

[1] Preface to the *Works*, quoted from the edition of 1668.

Cowley believed that the problem of making a synthesis of science and poetry was simple, and equally simple was the adaptation of religious themes to poetry. His was a mind that confused the statement of a problem with its solution. His own verse fails lamentably to discover any fresh way. He wrote his elaborate and rhetorical odes in support of the new science, and in condemnation of the imagination, which he sees in decay. So he contented himself that he had adjusted poetry to the new world of thought.

Among those whom Cowley praised in extending his welcome to the new science was Thomas Hobbes: the 'great *Columbus* of the *Golden Lands* of *new* Philosophies'. Had Cowley studied more closely the mind of this 'great Columbus' he might have been less sanguine about the future of poetry. In discussing the conflict of 'reason' and 'imagination' Hobbes invented little, but he restated Bacon's conclusions with the arid mathematical precision typical of his thought. Bacon, even if his argument attacked the imagination and poetry, had still in his style the gesture of magnificence. Hobbes makes up the account of poetry like some dusty clerk, and finds the balance on the wrong side. The poet has ever been willing to admit powers which he cannot comprehend but which yet render themselves serviceable to his art. For Hobbes there is within the mind nothing unknown, no half lights. He will illuminate everything in the hard unchanging white monotony of his prose. So in *Humane Nature* he writes: 'So soon as ever by turning aside of the Organs the *Object ceaseth* to work, that is to say, though the *Sense* be *past*, the *Image* or conception *remaineth*; but more *obscure* while we are *awake,* because some *object* or other continually *plieth* and solliciteth our Eyes and Ears, *keeping* the Minde in a *stronger* motion, whereby the *weaker* doth *not* easily *appear*. And this obscure conception is that we call Phantasie, or Imagination: Imagination being (to define it) *conception remaining, and by little and little decaying from and after the act of Sense*.'

Hobbes elaborated his attack on the pretensions of the imagination in a friendly controversy with Sir William Davenant, and their findings affect a number of minds in the later seventeenth century, particularly Dryden's. Davenant, like Cowley, had felt that the older mythology could no longer serve as a basis for poetry in a world of science and reason. Like Cowley he felt that the only solution remaining lay in the composition of a Christian poem. He has this advantage over Cowley that he sees more clearly the difficulty of the adjustments which he wishes to make, though he shares with Cowley an inability to create the poetry which his critical principles directed him to write. His position appears clearly in a passage on Tasso in the preface to *Gondibert*: 'For though the elder Poets (which were then the sacred Priests) fed the world with supernatural Tales, and so compounded the Religion, of Pleasure and Mysterie, (two Ingredients which never fail'd to work upon the People)—a Christian Poet, whose Religion little needs the aids of Invention, hath less occasion to imitate such Fables—and make a resemblance of Hell, out of the Dreams of frighted Women.' To this Hobbes had replied with an elaboration of Bacon's argument: 'Time and education begets experience; Experience begets Memory: Memory begets Judgement: Judgement begets the strength and structure, and Fancy begets the ornaments of a Poem.' Davenant's own honest but dreary *Gondibert* was the attempt of a writer of talent to set these theories into a poem, and the verses commending his attempt show how far the recession from imagination and mythology was accepted by contemporary minds. Edmund Waller wrote of *Gondibert*:

> Which no bold tales of Gods and Monsters swell
> But human passions such as with us dwell.

Cowley took the opportunity of elaborating an argument which he had developed elsewhere:

> Methinks *Heroick Poesie*, till now
> Like some fantastick *Fairy-Land* did show,
> *Gods, Devils, Nymphs, Witches*, and *Giants* Race,
> And all but *Man*, in Man's *Chief* work had place.
> Thou like some worthy *Knight* with Sacred Arms
> Dost drive the *Monsters* hence, and end the *Charms*.

Here in the later seventeenth century is found a crucial development in English poetry, not so much for what is achieved but in the mental change towards poetry. The dilemma arises not from a conflict of schools of verse, certainly not from a contrast of romantic and classical, but with greater inevitability from the difference between the older world of the imagination and the world as it is subdued by science and reason. That the issue is not conceived in classical and romantic terms can be seen in the rejection by Cowley and Davenant both of the world of mythology and of chivalry. The territory of poetry is being hedged off from life, or at least from the serious purposes of life as Bacon conceived them. The poet is welcome to develop a world apart, not a world of much importance, fanciful, erratic, a place of shadows. The invitation to the romantic terrain is extended first to the poet by the scientist or by the philosophers who have a respect for science. The only serious purpose left to the poet is the conversion of the Christian story into epic, but though Cowley and Davenant discuss this aim, and even attempt it, neither succeeds.

The dilemma is the most critical with which poetry in the modern period has been faced, and many aspects of the problem remain unsolved. Yet, as has already appeared, our English poetry has been continually successful in effecting a compromise. In this period when aridity threatens our verse Milton appears, and with a supreme adjustment of intellect with poetic genius succeeds in great measure in overcoming the problem. He introduces a wealth and magnificence into the poetic tradition by a happy union of much that lay in the past of poetry and was forgotten with the necessities of the contemporary outlook. Nothing has been more unjust in recent criticism than the attack on Milton which has accompanied the elevation of Donne. The hostility has been accompanied by an absence of historical perspective. For it was after the discussions of Cowley and Davenant and Hobbes, and of the many that sympathized with them, that Milton published his epic poems and his tragedy. His appearance at that time was fortunate for poetry but difficult for the poet. Shakespeare was supremely lucky in the period of his emergence as a poet; he was able to draw strength from the age and the society around him. So could Milton in his youth and in his middle age, but when he came to his epics and the tragedy he had to pit his mind in isolation against a society and a mental atmosphere hostile to his purposes. While poetry was being driven into submission to science and reason Milton had re-asserted its greatness and its divine origin: 'these abilities (of a poet) wheresoever they be found, are the inspired gift of God, rarely bestow'd.'[1] Verse was not one of the daughters of Memory, but, transcending reason, reminded man of the divine in his origins:

> Verse is work divine; despise not thou
> Verse therefore; which evinces (nothing more)
> Man's heavenly source, and which, retaining still
> Some scintillations of Promethean fire
> Bespeaks him animated from above.[2]

Nor was he less certain that he himself possessed this divine gift of poetry. 'Lastly,' he writes in reference to the prose of one of his pamphlets, 'I should not choose this manner of writing, wherein knowing my self inferior to my self, led by the genial power of nature to another task, I have the use, as I may account it, but of my left hand.'[3]

He had looked back over the past of poetry and understood, as no one else in his time, the purposes of Spenser, to serve his country under God by his verse. He had looked back too to the Renaissance in Italy, to Italian literature and criticism, for the conception of the profession of poetry, and its high purposes. Beyond Italy he looked to Greece and to the literature of the Hebrews. The dull confines set up by Hobbes he overleaped as easily as Satan into paradise, and setting for his purpose the construction of poems which should bring into English poetry all the best of form and structure of

[1] *Reason of Church Government*, Bk. II.
[2] *Ad Patrem.* Cowper's translation.
[3] *Reason of Church Government*, Bk. II.

the Ancients he welcomed mythology back into his verse.

To achieve his purpose he was driven to cut himself apart. On the growing popularity of the couplet he made a stabbing comment in the preface to *Paradise Lost*. He had anticipated Hobbes's reference to memory as the mother of the Muses and affirmed another conception of poetry: 'Neither do I think it shame to covenant with any knowing reader, that for some few years yet I may go on trust with him toward the payment of what I am now indebted, as being a work not to be raised from the heat of youth, or the vapours of wine, like that which flows at waste from the pen of some vulgar Amourist, or the trencher fury of a riming parasite; nor to be obtained by the invocation of Dame Memory and her Siren daughters, but by devout prayer to that eternal Spirit who can enrich with all utterance and knowledge, and sends out his Seraphim, with the hallowed fire of his Altar to touch and purify the lips of whom he pleases.'[1] The poets who had gathered around Davenant to praise him for his *Gondibert* had commended the conception of a religious poem. Milton accepted this challenge. If there was to be a Christian epic it should be not in the way of *Davideis* or *Gondibert* but on the more generous plan of *Paradise Lost*.

He was conscious of his own purposes and conscious also of a conflict with the purposes of his age. The result, as often in our poetic tradition, was a compromise, and the degree of the compromise can be measured by the difference between Milton's original aim and his achievement. In design he owed everything to classical theory, and unlike Spenser he mastered his

[1] *The Reason of Church Government*, etc., Bk. II.

preconceived plan. In no writer was the intellect so alert in the service of the imagination. This classical form has often disguised what it contains. It is true that he has accepted the conception that in theme the poem shall be Christian, but the biblical story is only the central design in an emblazonry which includes Greek mythology, medieval and popular lore and his own invention. So among the fallen spirits Mulciber can be discovered, described in telling lines which Keats later was to recall and employ:

> Men call'd him *Mulciber*; and how he fell
> From Heav'n they fabl'd, thrown by angry *Jove*
> Sheer o're the Chrystal Battlements: from Morn
> To Noon he fell, from Noon to dewy Eve,
> A Summers day; and with the setting Sun
> Dropt from the Zenith like a falling Star,
> On *Lemnos*, th' Ægean Ile.

The witchcraft and folklore are affixed by Gothic additions to the classical design:

> Nor uglier follow the Night-Hag, when call'd
> In secret, riding through the Air she comes
> Lur'd with the smell of infant blood, to dance
> With *Lapland* Witches, while the labouring Moon
> Eclipses at thir charms.

Sometimes he would glance back regretfully at the Arthurian theme which he had once thought possible. The regret must have been the keener if, as E. M. W. Tillyard suggests, he had hoped for such a transformation at the beginning of the Parliamentary régime that it could be commended in an epic on the Arthurian theme. Sir Walter Scott wished that he had chosen an Arthurian story,[1] and it was in the terms of chivalry that Dryden often thought of Milton's epic: 'if the giant had not foiled the knight, and driven him out of his stronghold, to wander through the world with his lady errant.'[2] Even if he could not use the stories of the romances, he remembered them:

> and what resounds
> In Fable or *Romance* of *Uthers* Son
> Begirt with *British* and *Armoric* Knights;
> And all who since, Baptiz'd or Infidel
> Jousted in *Aspramont* or *Montalban*,
> *Damasco*, or *Marocco*, or *Trebisond*,
> Or whom *Biserta* sent from *Afric* shore
> When *Charlemain* with all his Peerage fell
> By *Fontarabbia*.

In language he did not conform to a manner which has much similarity or sympathy with a classical style. He had, like each great poet, achieved individuality. In the early poems a number of influences could be detected, even at times the methods of Donne. The mature work shows direct influence only rarely, though it is rich in recollections classical and native. With all the differences which his individual genius imposed on his treatment of vocabulary, his verse returned to the adorned tradition of Spenser and Shakespeare, and away from the abrupt realism and natural speech rhythms of Donne. The classical virtues of directness and clarity he seldom aimed at, despite any indebtedness in vocabulary to words of classical origin. His purposes carry him away rather to dim, half-seen effects, as Burke was

[1] See Preface to *King Arthur*, 1808.
[2] *A Discourse of Epick Poetry*.

to note later in the *Sublime and Beautiful*, suggestions rather than direct descriptions, to phrases which carry along with them all the mystery of the unknown:

>No light, but rather darkness visible

or

>With ever-burning Sulphur unconsum'd.

The poet whose aim had been classical was led into methods in language which were often similar to those of the later romantic poets.

Nowhere has recent criticism been more unjust than in the condemnation of Milton's style, though the balance is somewhat restored by Sir Herbert Grierson's defence in *Milton and Wordsworth*, though Sir Herbert seems sometimes to place the best of Wordsworth against the worst of Milton. Milton cannot be assessed, as some modern critics seem to imply, by saying that he did not write like Dryden. Their purposes were different, but when Dryden approached heroic poetry in *Absalom and Achitophel* he showed how profitably he had studied Milton. Nor can Milton be condemned for the eighteenth-century imitators whose work is always complicated by the fact that it began in parody. On greater poets than these, on Wordsworth and on Keats, his influence works out more beneficially. Wordsworth matured a blank verse of his own, but it has the signs of his affection for Milton, while all the evidence leads to the rejection of Keats's statement that he abandoned *Hyperion* from a sense of the unhappy effects of Milton's influence.[1] Still less would it be just to isolate the more argumentative passages in *Paradise*

---

[1] I examine the evidence in *Keats*, 1934.

Lost and generalize from these. Milton's great invention is his creation of a style suitable for a cosmic and heroic poem, the greatest poem in English which has an action and characters, and conversations, and which through its imagery touches upon life illimitably.

The character of Satan is the supreme instance in our poetry of the meeting of the classical and romantic. Whatever may have been Milton's intentions, he fashioned out in Satan a figure of rebellion at which later romanticists were to rejoice. Where in French literature can an example be found of Racine or Voltaire providing a model, even if it is to be considered an unintentional model, for later, romantic or even decadent writers! Whether Milton realized the emphasis which he was giving will remain a matter of dispute. E. H. Visiak has suggested[1] that Satan was a dream of Milton's thwarted purposes and E. M. W. Tillyard adds, 'the character of Satan expresses, as no other character or act or feature of the poem does, something in which Milton believed very strongly: heroic energy'.[2] To suggest that Milton consciously favoured or approved of his Satan is absurd. What happened was that the pattern of the action, considered as an abstract pattern, the conflict of individuals against a totalitarian authority, conformed to a pattern in Milton's own life with Milton himself on the rebel's side. The identity of the patterns led to the glamour and magnificence which surrounds Satan in the early parts of the epic, before the theological purpose more securely asserts itself. The influence of the Miltonic Satan was one which the poet could certainly not have anticipated. He became, with Macbeth,

[1] *Milton Agonistes*, 1923.
[2] *Milton*, 1930.

a pattern for those who valued their own passions and sensibilities above a loyalty to the moral world in which they found themselves. *Lara* and the *Giaour* are formed ultimately on the model of Milton's Satan, and so, in part, is the poet who made them.

The result is that in English poetry the two great non-dramatic poems constructed with a formal classical pattern have left an influence on later poetry far removed from the original intentions of the poets who composed them: Spenser, who would make a 'poem historical' and so serve his Queen and his country by the creation of a moral order for society, left a territory of romance: Milton who would 'justify the ways of God to man' erected a figure which in one disguise or another became the justification of the individual questing for experience. With Milton as distinct from Spenser there remained the intellectual triumph over form, which Dryden admired and in part imitated. As a result, in the middle of the age when science looked askance at poetry and attempted to lessen its esteem as opposed to 'Reason' English poetry achieved a great poem, fashioned of many memories, but formally the closest approach to that idea of an epic poem which had so long engaged the attention of powerful minds.

V

DRYDEN AND POPE

DRYDEN was Milton's younger contemporary and his admirer. With him there developed the verse in English which answers most fully to the definitions of classical, the heroic couplet as it is found in him, and later in Pope and Johnson. Further, he had more than any preceding poet the desire and capacity to express himself in criticism. Dryden, as Johnson comments, writes 'the criticism of a poet'. In his critical essays he is seeking out the results that will help him in his own work. This can be discovered as his consistent purpose, despite the fact that an interest in critical reading, and sometimes even the pressure of composition, led him occasionally to derived and less well-considered judgments. 'Spenser wanted only to have read the rules of Bossu' is Dryden writing in his sleep, though this time he woke up before the end of the sentence, adding, 'for no man was ever born with a greater genius, or had more knowledge to support it.'[1]

It is with Dryden that the difference between the English and French tradition in classicism becomes most distinctly apparent. Dryden had a respect for tradition, for the rules, and even for French 'correctness'. But in between Spenser and Dryden there lay the drama of

[1] *A Discourse on Epick Poetry.*

Shakespeare and Ben Jonson, and in non-dramatic poetry, Milton with his strangely conflicting purposes. All this Dryden is far too alert and honest to ignore. Sometimes a temporary enthusiasm for Rapin, or Bossu, or Mr. Rymer leads him to exclaim at Shakespeare's irregularities, but the mood cannot last long, for the genuine praise returns for one who 'had, undoubtedly, a larger soul of poesy than ever any of our nation'.[1] Dryden's awareness of a number of different ways in poetry and his tolerance bewilder a French classical critic such as Voltaire. In the dedication to *Zaïre*, Voltaire found Dryden sufficiently acceptable to describe him as 'un très grand génie', though he is troubled by 'des hyperboles de rhétorique, ou des indécences' in the Heroic dramas. In the *Lettres Philosophiques* he defines him as 'auteur plus fécond que judicieux'.

Dryden, like every writer, draws part of his vision from the condition of literature and the general atmosphere of ideas in his time. His individual quality lies in his attempt, during a period when this contemporary pressure was urgent, to seek enlightenment from past tradition. Despite his admiration for classicism he refuses in all his most original critical work to equate tradition with an adherence to the prescriptions of the 'rules'. At times he is dominated by them and ever they have his respect, but for him tradition is more widely the practice of what he considers best in the past. This leads him finally to the wholly delightful praise of Chaucer as compared with Ovid in the *Preface to the Fables*, but the same wise tolerance instructs him at the moments of most awakened insight throughout his critical work. He is led, more explicitly than any of

[1] *Epistle Dedicatory to the Rival Ladies.*

his predecessors and in the face of greater temptations, to that middle road which has been typical of English poetry since Chaucer. Not only in the debate on the 'rules' did he find his way through. More than most in his age he appreciated the new science, but he is equally secure in facing the strictures of the Royal Society on the language for poetry. In a magnificent passage in *A Discourse on Epick Poetry*, with Horace to aid him, he answers those who would remove from poetic vocabulary all that surpassed the necessities of bare statement: 'I trade both with the living and the dead, for the enrichment of our native language. We have enough in England to supply our necessity; but if we will have things of magnificence and splendour, we must get them by commerce. Poetry requires ornament, and that is not to be had from our old Teuton monosyllables; therefore, if I find an elegant word in a classick author, I propose it to be naturalized by using it myself; and if the publick approves of it, the bill passes.'

Of Dryden's delight in classical literature, his own testimony stands, given often and emphatically though never with more conviction than in the dedication of *Troilus and Cressida*: 'I am often put to a stand in considering whether what I write be the idiom of the tongue, or false grammar, and nonsense couched beneath that specious name of *Anglicism*: and have no other way to clear my doubts but by translating my English into Latin, and thereby trying, what sense the words will bear in a more stable tongue.' In a narrower way it was Dryden who made the reputation of Boileau in England by his translation in 1683, with Sir William Soames. On the other hand, it was Dryden who first gave currency to the term 'create' in contrast to the older, classical term, 'imitate'. The passage occurs in the *Preface* to *Troilus and Cressida*: 'Caliban, or the Monster in THE TEMPEST. He seems there to have created a person which was not in nature, a boldness which, at first sight, would appear intolerable.' The terms 'create' and 'creative', used in a more specialized and restrictive sense it is true, were later to become the most distinctive counters in romantic criticism. Again it was Dryden, employing a vocabulary derived from Hobbes, who first gave an account of the poet's activity, akin to those found in contemporary theories of the unconscious. In the *Epistle Dedicatory* to *The Rival Ladies* he writes: 'Fancy was yet in its first work, moving the sleeping images of things towards the light, there to be distinguished, and then either chosen or rejected by the judgment. . . . I confess, in that first tumult of my thoughts, there appeared a disorderly kind of beauty in some of them—but I was then in that eagerness of imagination, which by over-pleasing fanciful men, flatters them into the danger of writing.' Dryden delighted in 'decorum', and yet Dryden provided the extravagant and romantic sentiment of the heroic plays. Nor, despite his interests in a classical precision in language, could he prevent the spaniel from wandering far over the field of memory: 'for imagination in a poet is a faculty so wild and lawless that, like an high-ranging spaniel, it must have clogs tied to it, lest it outrun the judgment.' The whole development of the poetry which follows, the most classical in our literature, is affected by the fact that at its front stands the far-reaching and tolerant criticism of Dryden.

In poetry he did not achieve all that he wished. Economic motives kept him too long in the theatre, and for a large part of that time he was occupied with the pathological development of heroic plays. The quality of the verse in those plays has often been underestimated. It can best be judged, like the verse of Swinburne's dramas, in individual passages, penetrating and skilful, but woven into a general texture which is unsound. His ambition was to give to his country an epic poem, which he once described as 'undoubtedly the greatest work which the soul of man is capable to perform'.[1] This he never accomplished, and so the school which is closest to classicism in English poetry begins in satire, and never extends with much success beyond satire or discursive verse. He set the tradition of poetry on this narrower basis, not intentionally but through circumstance. His genuine service to English verse lay in his discipline of 'numbers'. His only approach to great narrative, apart from incidental passages in the satires, lay in translation. In rendering Virgil his major motive was economic, but, as he wrote to Dennis, he wished to show that 'no man is fit to write after him in a barbarous modern tongue'. Had circumstances been different he would himself have ventured: 'some little hopes', he wrote in the dedication to *Aurengzebe*, 'I have yet remaining (and those too, considering my abilities, may be vain), that I may make the world some part of amends for many ill plays, by an heroick poem.'

Dryden's failure to achieve an epic or heroic poem, while it may be ascribed largely to circumstances, cannot be completely so explained. He inherited the problem of Donne and of Davenant, the inadequacy of the older mythologies and his inability to discover a new one.

[1] *A Discourse on Epick Poetry.*

That the subject was of dominant interest to him can be seen apart from a number of other passages in a long digression on epic poetry in the *Discourse on the Origin and Progress of Satire.* He had been impressed by Boileau's argument that the Christian poet had no machinery to supply the place of that found in Homer or in Virgil. He admitted that the Christian virtues, consisting 'in patience and suffering, for the love of God whatever hardships can befall the world', would lead to an introspective poetry not to a poetry of action. For his own part, he still conceives the great epic poem possible, but in some of these passages he seems to foresee the poetry which more than a century later would appear in Wordsworth supremely and in Shelley and Keats, where either by direct description, or interpreted through mythology the poet's own experience would constitute the centre of the poem. Dryden could not himself conceive of poetry in that way; he desired an action, as in classical epic, with an opportunity to present manners and society, and with possibly the background of a supernatural world. No wonder that he looked almost enviously at Milton's achievements. He had plans of his own to offer, though he knew that they could not be fulfilled. He suggested how scenes from the Old Testament might be adapted to epic purposes, or 'King Arthur conquering the Saxons', or 'Edward the Black Prince, in subduing Spain and restoring it to the lawful prince, though a great tyrant, Don Pedro the Cruel'. Whether any of these 'rude draughts' of what he had 'been long labouring in his imagination' would have had success may be doubted, but Johnson was later to lament that Dryden did not attempt one of them.

He excused himself by the financial necessity of working for the stage, by the fact that King Charles had encouraged him 'only with fair words': 'my little salary ill paid, and no prospect of a future subsistance, I was then discouraged in the beginning of my attempt; and now age has overtaken me, and want, a more insufferable evil, through the change of the times, has slowly disenabled me'. Beyond this there remained the fact that Dryden, like Scott later, had a wide-ranging genius without a depth of individual vision. As T. S. Eliot has written: 'Dryden lacked what his master Jonson possessed, a large and unique view of life; he lacked insight, he lacked profundity.'[1] He gave to poetry much that was original. In *Annus Mirabilis*, an under-estimated piece, and in *Absalom and Achitophel*, he showed how contemporary circumstance could be rendered poetically. Further, whatever the histories of literature may quote of antecedents, he invented English satire. Despite his insight in the critical essays, in his verse he surrendered poetry to reason and to actuality. The reward was a poetry widely read and fully intelligible, and beyond that a tradition in poetry more classical than any other in our literature. The great ambition of the epic poem however was not accomplished, but only discussed in the prose essays and that consideration narrows the perfection of what was to follow.

Dryden's example had suggested the surrender of imagination to reason, and that example influenced Pope. A poetry resulted, so widely intelligible that its appreciation has been one of the most genuine and widespread in the whole history of our non-dramatic verse, extending from the eighteenth century into the

[1] *Selected Essays*, 1932.

nineteenth. Sir William Dyott, aide-de-camp to George III, as an old man in 1832, recalled at Clivedon Park that he was on the site of the house of the Duke of Buckingham, 'famed by Pope in his essay on riches'.[1] Dyott's reference is the more notable because he has few literary reminiscences in his diary. Rogers could remember the boatman who as a boy had seen Mr. Pope seated in his sedan-chair as he was rowed up the Thames. The opinions on the decline of Pope's reputation in the eighteenth century come from prejudiced parties who wished to see it decline. Aaron Hill writing to Samuel Richardson in 1744 comments on 'the wane of his popularity', but Aaron Hill thought meanly of Pope: 'he had a turn for verse, without a soul for poetry. He stuck himself into his subjects, and his muse partook his maladies; which, with a kind of peevish and vindictive consciousness, maligned the healthy and the satisfied.'[2] Against such paltry criticism the record of editions alone will prove that Pope was admired continuously for a century and more, and admired widely in the early nineteenth century when some younger writers such as Keats were so outspoken against him.

The seventeenth century, from Donne and Milton to Dryden, was, as has been suggested, the critical period for the development of poetry. Pope had not the complexity of Dryden's position, for largely he accepted Dryden's solution. His religion was Catholic, and though it troubled him seldom, it kept him free from one of Dryden's dilemmas. The new science, to which

[1] *Sir W. Dyott*, ed. R. W. Jeffrey, 1907.
[2] *The Correspondence of Samuel Richardson*, ed. Barbauld, London, 1804. Vol. I, 106.

Dryden had given a genuine and understanding tribute, was beyond his range. If anything he was antagonistic, not from any deep purpose, but as an aftermath of Scriblerus talks with Swift. His achievement, even in literature, was narrower. He wrote some prose criticism, his letters, the Homer and the Shakespeare prefaces, but he never possessed Dryden's way of ferreting after a difficult argument until a conclusion was reached. The drama occupied him, except incidentally, only as an editor. In non-dramatic poetry he shared with Dryden an admiration for the epic, as the supreme poetic form. It was a purpose he was to achieve only through translation, and, most significantly, in mock-heroic, in *The Rape of the Lock*. Within this narrower range there were purposes which he could excellently serve, the perfection of diction, the portraiture of society and the correction of taste. No poet worked more consistently towards one end or gained his preconceived intentions so securely. It is true that he was distracted into 'the quarrels of authors' and the punishment of Dunces, but even here the central purpose is never lost entirely. The perspicacity of his mind is early illustrated in his *Essay on Criticism*. One of the most derived poems in the language, it is yet one of the most self-revealing. Commentators have shown how the ideas, sometimes even the verbal recollections, derive from Horace, from Boileau's *L'Art Poétique* and from the translation of Boileau by Soames and Dryden. When all has been conceded the poem is not a patchwork, but a clear pronouncement of principles, Pope's own guide to his later work.

He had learned from Boileau a more important lesson than the critical principles derived from Horace.

From Boileau's *Le Lutrin* he had seen the way to mock-heroic, where all his thought and love for the epic could be played out in a framework of contemporary incident and satiric intention. Here, exquisitely adjusted to his dilemma, was the appropriate solution, not the ardours and endeavours of genuine epic structure with which Milton had matched himself, but the intellectual pattern isolated and exposed for appreciation. Without Boileau he might have been led to burlesque, to the shapeless, instead of preserving in *The Rape of the Lock* a supreme precision of form. Exquisite in itself, this could give poetry no new direction as Spenser or Milton had done. It derived its strength from a nobler conception. He had reduced mythology to the sylphs; dissociated it from great action; controlled it and rendered it acceptable to the reason through parody. *The Rape of the Lock* is part of the farewell to mythology which limited the purposes of eighteenth-century poetry. That this was understood by his contemporaries can be seen from a passage in *The Spectator*.[1] 'In mock heroic poems the use of the heathen mythology is not only excusable, but graceful, because it is the design of such compositions to divert, by adapting the fabulous machines of the ancients to low subjects, and at the same time by ridiculing such kinds of machinery in modern writers.' But myth is not suitable for 'our serious compositions'.

In his 'serious compositions' Pope answers to more definitions of the classical than any other English writer. He did not attach to poetry in general, certainly not to his own compositions, the high importance and sense of dedication to be found in Wordsworth or Shelley, nor would he have supported the ideal which Sidney had

[1] No. 523, 30 October, 1712.

advocated in the *Apologie*. Life itself, and in life, good conduct, and, as conduct touched upon art, the exercise of good taste, these were the vital matters, and poetry should serve them. It only obscures the issue to suggest that in the letters and the vituperative passages in the poems, he departed from these standards. He was a strangely complex personality, baffled, thwarted, with a rich vein of suppressed sentiment. But wherever his reason directed him, it was towards this standard of good taste and good living. As the conclusion to *The Dunciad* shows, he was too close to Swift to have any bold hopes for humanity. Under another influence equally powerful but more genial, he might have developed differently. The early poems, the *Pastorals*, and *Windsor Forest*, and even some passages in *An Essay on Criticism* suggest that he was sensitive towards nature and had desires at times to move in an imaginary world. Without Swift, and without the quarrel with Ambrose Philips over the *Pastorals*, he might have been led to create an imaginary world to fill out the inadequacies of the present life. When he did approach sentiment, or the other world of medievalism, in the *Elegy to an Unfortunate Lady* and in *Eloisa to Abelard* he had a less secure hold of his vocabulary and even upon the couplet itself. But the rococo beauty of *The Rape of the Lock* showed that he had longings for something outside the mere form and fashion of contemporary life.

If he stated his purposes in *An Essay on Criticism* it was in the Epistles and Satires that he matured them. The result is that English classicism, as it is represented in Pope and those who follow him, does not imitate any great poem of action. Byron, in one of his more extravagant eulogies of Pope, wrote that 'the highest of all poetry is ethical poetry, as the highest of all earthly objects must be moral truth'. To accept this is to limit the range and capability of poetry itself. Courthope, one of the fairest critics of the eighteenth century, realized this clearly: 'Many persons in the eighteenth century thought, with Marmontel, that "the end of the didactic poem is to instruct"; whereas the true end of all poetry is to please. The rank of a poem depends on the kind of pleasure it produces, and no instructed judge would maintain, on reflection, that the imaginative pleasure produced by ethical compositions like Horace's *Satires* and *Epistles* can compare in quality with the pleasure arising out of simple narratives of action, such as Homer's *Iliad*.'[1] The strength of Pope lies in his consistent adherence to his own aim, whatever his limitations, real and alleged, may be.

The *Essay on Man*, with its superficial optimism, may seem to contradict these conclusions drawn from the rest of his mature work. But this poem has been misjudged in the same way as the *Essay on Criticism*. Its central theme is derived, and the method is discursive, but underlying this there are other elements. Much in the poem had come facilely from Bolingbroke, and from Shaftesbury's *Characteristics*, and remained mere argument unconverted into poetry. Deeper than this was the view of man which Pope held consistently. No less than in *The Dunciad* or in the Epistles and Satires he portrayed in the poem an image of man, limited by his own powers, tempted to vanity by pride, and capable of good only by modesty, and discipline and tradition:

  Plac'd on the Isthmus of a Middle State,
  A Being darkly wise, and rudely great.

[1] *A History of English Poetry*, Vol. V., p. 284.

On the one side lay the temptation to fall back merely to an animal state, and this Pope was near enough to Swift to see only too clearly:

> Fix'd like a Plant on his peculiar Spot,
> To draw Nutrition, propagate, and rot.

On the other side beckoned the ambition of the romantic, the solution of Byron over the 'lazar-house of human woes' and this Pope envisioned with equal insight:

> Or Meteor-like, flame lawless through the Void,
> Destroying others by himself destroy'd.

These illuminating if incidental passages in *An Essay on Man* show that Pope maintained the view which Swift held so passionately that man, despite his pride, was insignificant. He shared with many minds in the early eighteenth century a sense of modesty which made him self-conscious of sensibility, and diffident of the vaunting ambitions of the imagination. This modesty, which contrasted with his superficial arrogance, arose in part from an awareness of what science, particularly astronomical science, was maintaining. With Pope the realization is never profound, but it is present none the less. Man under the old Ptolemaic system, when the earth was the centre of the universe and he the noblest of earth's creatures, had a much more solid motive for pride than when the Copernican system showed him insecurely fixed on possibly one of the less significant of the planets. Pope as he approached life had a modesty to which none of the romantics attained. As he approached nature he could not bring himself to believe that it was created solely to decorate his moods:

> Has God, thou Fool! work'd solely for thy Good,
> Thy Joy, thy Pastime, thy Attire, thy Food?
> Who for thy Table feeds the wanton Fawn
> For him as kindly spread the Flow'ry Lawn.
> Is it for thee the Lark ascends and sings?
> Joy tunes his Voice, Joy elevates his Wings?

While he determined the course which his own poetry was to follow, Pope was not bitter or antagonistic to the great writers of the past who had held to other ways. In his attack on Timon's villa, his final thrust is that it will be useless to look there for Milton's works. He had vituperation enough for the Grub Street writers, for editors, for critics, but not for the great that preceded him:

> Ev'n such small Critics some regard may claim,
> Preserv'd in Milton's or in Shakespeare's name.

If he produced a poetry that was classical he had at times almost a longing for some other manner. *The Rape of the Lock* can ultimately only be understood in the light of that realization. The couplet which he selected as his favourite from all his verse is one which has the illimitable suggestion of romantic poetry.

> Lo, Where Mæotis sleeps, and hardly flows
> The freezing Tanais thro' a waste of snows.[1]

Pope, despite these gestures, made his poetry serve tradition, and reason, and ethics, constructing his narrow but perfected classical conception. In some strange way it has been assumed that the eighteenth century followed him. There is no second Pope in the eighteenth century. He has only one genuine successor, Samuel

---

[1] *Dunciad*, III, 87. Johnson in his life of Pope quotes the lines as the couplet by which Pope's own ear was 'most gratified'.

Johnson: for Goldsmith, though he may derive technically from Pope, has moved far in principles and methods. Even the tyranny of the couplet is an invention of criticism, for blank verse flourished with Thomson even in Pope's proudest years. The eighteenth century might indeed have fared better had the classical tradition been set on a wider basis and been longer maintained. As it is, the so-called age of reason, or age of prose, is actually the period of the growth of those sensibilities to which the name 'romantic' is to be later attached. Even Johnson, who admired Pope, and followed him, opened the door in his dramatic criticism to the excesses of romanticism. Not all is ordered and classical in the eighteenth century. Standards are confused, and at times the claims of criticism and the productions of writers are more excessive and grotesque than at any preceding period. Only when this is understood, and the false phrase 'pre-romanticism', removed, can the true and varied intentions of poetry in the early nineteenth century be rightly understood.

VI

THE EIGHTEENTH CENTURY

POPE had surrendered poetry to reason and throughout the eighteenth century Pope remained popular. Early in the century there was a realization that outside reason there was a world which must be mistrusted, however pleasurable. In 1712, the *Faerie Queene* is described in the *Spectator* as, 'a Fairyland where knights-errant have a full Scope to range and to do even what Ariostos or Orlandos might not do in the world without breaking into Credibility'.[1] From Donne onwards poets held aloof from this world beyond credibility, but the realization of its existence remained. In the early eighteenth century, while Pope's clear 'tessellated' couplets reveal the world of reason and order, the references to this secret world continue: 'the waking man is conversant in the world of nature: when he sleeps he retires to a private world that is particular to himself.'[2] This 'private world', where one had full scope without 'breaking into Credibility', enlarged itself in the eighteenth century. Despite all the attacks of the new science, and under the sober eye of enlightenment it developed its own literature, though it never informed a poet of the first magnitude.

[1] *Spectator*, No. 540, Wed., Nov. 19, 1712.
[2] *Spectator*, No. 487, Sept. 18, 1712.

THE EIGHTEENTH CENTURY 77

In the libraries of the great houses in the eighteenth century Mr. Pope's works were preserved and read, but in the very grounds of those houses there could often be found the dismembered relics of medievalism. At a little distance from the house of Sir Roger de Coverley lay the ruins of an old abbey, ghost-haunted, with a long walk of aged elms 'so very high, that when one passes under them, the Rooks and Crows that rest upon the Tops of them seem cawing in another Region'.[1] While the gentlemen of the eighteenth century might desire classical architecture in their own mansions, many of them found some strange memories aroused by these survivals of an older age within their grounds. If they studied the Palladian forms to be found in *Vitruvius Britannicus* they were also commissioning Samuel Buck to engrave in his elaborate volumes the ruined abbeys and castles which were now their private possessions within their parklands. Not only did they look with admiration towards the 'gothic', they recreated it and were content that it should stand side by side with classical structures: 'in the first quarter of the century Hawksmoor built the twin towers in the Quadrangle of All Souls' College in a mongrel Gothic style, and in 1737, only a few yards away, Gibbs began Radcliffe Camera, crowned with a dome that is first cousin of St. Paul's.'[2] From the early eighteenth century the 'classical' and this other element to be called first 'gothic' and later 'romantic' existed together. How closely together has been indicated by W. P. Ker in describing 'the successful hypocrisy of the Codrington Library of

[1] *Spectator*, No. 110, July 6, 1711.
[2] *Tides in English Taste* (1937), Vol. II, p. 68, by B. Sprague Allen.

All Souls—Gothic outside, to answer the fifteenth-century chapel on the other side of the quadrangle; inside, the perfect image of the eighteenth century in dignity and grace, unequalled'.[1]

To that other world of the imagination the eighteenth century found easy access through the remains of the middle ages which still lay so close to the modern world. Yet no one on retiring to that other world must forget that the solid, material world, governed by reason and good-sense, was of primary importance. If one were to forget, then Mr. Locke was close at hand with his chapter 'of the Association of Ideas', with the reminder that all these fancies owed their origin to the fact that in childhood ideas of goblins and sprites were associated with gloom and darkness.

The success of Samuel Buck's collection of engravings of the ruins of castles, abbeys, monasteries and palaces is an indication of this delight in something removed from plain good-sense of the contemporary world. Buck began his engravings in 1726, the year of Thomson's *Winter*, and he continued annually with his reproductions until the names of most of the gentry of England appear on the lists of his subscribers. Newstead Abbey is there in his collection for 1726, the great empty framework of its Gothic windows with the weeds growing around the crumbled edges of the stone. In 1732 Buck portrayed the north-east view of the ruins of Tintern, the broken pillars, the walls that never lead anywhere, the grass and even bushes growing from the broken surface, and again the empty framework of a window through which the owl can fly to rest in some ruined tower. The art of Claude and of Salvator Rosa was

[1] 'The Humanist Ideal': *Collected Essays*, Vol. II, 1925.

to help in linking this interest for the ruins of medievalism with a sensibility for external nature.

If medieval ruins were one means of awakening strange sensations and extravagant emotions another source of suggestion came from the merchants returning from the Orient, from India and China. Mrs. Philip Lybbe Powys on her progresses through England showed how varied and bizarre in the middle of the century were the tastes derived from these sources.[1] At Eastbury, in Dorset, at the Rt. Hon. George Dodington's she found marble tables 'out of one of the Italian palaces', and a Chinese bedroom 'furnish'd exactly as in China'. At Fawley Court, Bucks, she notes a bed-chamber 'with one of the finest red-ground chintz I ever saw, the panels of the room, painted, in each a different Chinese figure, larger than life'. At Lord de Despencer's church at West Wycombe she discovered 'a very superb Egyptian Hall, no pews, pulpit, or desk, except two ornamental seats which answer the two latter purposes: in fine it has only the appearance of a neat ballroom with rows of forms on each side'.

Extravagance of taste and of sentiment were seldom allowed to obscure the reality of the ordinary world. That it could be combined with severe moral judgments and with a refusal to accept any irregularity and radicalism in politics can be seen from Elizabeth Carter.[2] On Rousseau's *La Nouvelle Heloïse* she could write: 'no doubt finely writ, but one of the most dangerous and wicked books, in many respects, that I believe ever was published.' The *Confessions* she would not read: 'Indeed I soon found his writings of so bad a tendency

[1] *Diaries*, ed. E. J. Climenson, 1899.
[2] *Memoirs*, 2 vols, 1808.

that after a few trials, I determined never to look into anything he should publish. He always appeared to me a bad man. That he was mad I never doubted.' Away from reason was a removed tract where 'gothic' sensibility could have its free play. To her friend, Mrs. Vesey, she writes: 'You are now at leisure to amuse yourself with those enchanting scenes which your imagination is always ready to present to you whenever you bid it wave its magic wand. I am inexpressibly delighted with your Gothic retirement, which I shall certainly visit every moonlight evening; and I hope you will advance to meet me with the first ray, which you discover gleaming through your cathedral window. I am indeed a little apprehensive that you will make some scruple of admitting my vacant round face to so solemn an entertainment; but if you can once get over this mere prejudice of appearance, you will find me a very tractable companion and ready to follow your imagination wherever it will lead me "through the dark postern of time long elapsed". When the twilight aids the visions of contemplation and the owl begins his melancholy serenade, we will conjure up the Lady Abbess, and fix her in her niche in the wall.' With Elizabeth Carter, as with so many others, this desire for a 'gothic' play—world arose from contemplating the medieval ruins attached to the great private houses. Her letters refer constantly to the 'gothic' delight of ruins, found in the ancient seats which she visits, 'the venerable buildings', 'the arches dimly lighted by pale lamps', the broken towers, and chapels: they all arouse in her emotions in which she luxuriates.

If there are tendencies in English taste which correspond to the more extreme definitions of romanticism, given by Mario Praz,[1] it is in the eighteenth century that they are to be found. They are never dominant, for they synchronize with the age of good-sense and with the popularity of Pope's poetry. They never gain notable poetic expression, though in Beckford and Horace Walpole they find their way into prose fiction. The Beckford family is an interesting example of the conditions which permitted of the indulgence in these exotic sensations in the eighteenth century. William Beckford's ancestor early in the seventeenth century was 'sittizen and clothworker of Maidenhead'.[2] His son, Peter, migrated in Charles II's reign to Jamaica, where, with privateering and other activities, he amassed a solid fortune. Already in Jamaica the colonists had a delight 'in proud but tasteless magnificence, the tables and utensils were of silver, and the horses were sometimes shod with plates of the same metal, loosely nailed and carelessly dropped, to indicate their riders' contempt for their riches'. The second generation in Jamaica could produce a Governor for the Island and a fortune of half a million pounds. With the next generation the family reappeared in England and its most promising member emerged as a solid citizen, Lord Mayor of London and a Member of Parliament. He still had in every way the energy of the early members of the family and a fortune estimated as one of the greatest in England, plantations and slaves in the West Indies, lands in Wiltshire, Bedfordshire and London, a great mansion at Fonthill, near Shaftesbury, seven natural children and one legitimate child, his heir. William Beckford, with

[1] See page 1.
[2] *Beckford*, Guy Chapman, 1937: I am indebted to this volume in the pages which follow, from which all the quotations are taken.

this ancestry, leisured and without any settled tradition, fantastically wealthy, and gifted to the very verge of genius, could indulge to the extremities in the phantasies with which others only idly and occasionally dallied. 'What a strange animal I was in those days, abandoned to all the wildness of my imagination and setting no bounds to my caprices.' With Beckford it was no longer a Gothic solitude into which the mind could escape from reason, knowing reason still to exist. In him the phantasy became the reality. He was to be Vathek 'ninth Caliph of the race of the Abassides, the son of Montassem, and the grandson of Haroun-al-Raschid'.

Horace Walpole was different and more typical. His indulgence in 'Gothic' extravagancies was consciously effected, with his intelligence retaining a sound hold upon the sober values of the ordinary world. The contrast is illustrated in his single comment on Beckford that he had 'just parts enough to lead him astray from common sense'.[1] Walpole's letters show how varied his life had been, and with what a keen eye he watched everything that happened around him. Like Beckford he had a notable father behind him, and he had an income which allowed him to develop his own tastes: a more modest income than Beckford's, it is true, but more carefully husbanded, and if more modest still considerable, for by his own reckoning his sinecures were producing nearly two thousand pounds a year as early as 1744, while later the emoluments rose to double the value of this sum. He once wrote half-ironically that it was 'the marvellous, the eccentric, that characterizes Englishmen', and for himself he wished to build an

[1] 8 July, 1784.

atmosphere of his own, strange and remote, a private world, known to be unreal, yet enjoyable, where he could wander at will: 'Oh! with what joy I could bid adieu to loving and hating! to crowds, public places, great dinners, visits—and above all, to the House of Commons!—but pray mind, when I retire, it shall only be to London and Strawberry Hill—in London one can live as one will, and at Strawberry Hill I will live as I will.'[1] He had never the sense of a profound nostalgia for another world; his retreat was an indulgence, not a spiritual necessity. While he built the residence of Mrs. Chenevix, the toy-shop proprietress, into his castellated gothic residence of Strawberry Hill he was watching himself, even laughing at himself: 'a little plaything-house that I got out of Mrs. Chenevix's shop, and is the prettiest bauble you ever saw.'

Part of his mind was satisfied with Strawberry Hill as a game: 'a private world particular to himself', knowing only too well that the other world of public places, great dinners, and the House of Commons, existed. His antiquarianism was the most solid intellectual interest that supported him in this domain of his own will, but it left him not fully satisfied. The importance which he attached to *The Castle of Otranto* shows that he wanted something more, to recreate this past, and to unite it in some way with contemporary life. This dream-life of Strawberry Hill could not be made to remain a plaything, for it entered powerfully into his subconscious life: 'Shall I even confess to you, what was the origin of this romance? I waked one morning in the beginning of last June, from a dream, of

[1] 19 February, 1765: all quotations from Walpole's letters are from Mrs. Paget Toynbee's edition.

which, all I could recover was, that I had thought myself in an ancient castle (a very natural dream for a head filled like mine with Gothic story), and that on the uppermost banister of a great staircase I saw a gigantic hand in armour. In the evening I sat down, and began to write, without knowing in the least what I intended to say or relate. The work grew on my hands, and I grew fond of it—add that I was very glad to think of anything, rather than politics. . . . You will laugh at my earnestness, but if I have amused you, by retracing with any fidelity the manners of ancient days, I am content, and give you leave to think me as idle as you please.'[1] When *The Castle of Otranto* had been successful, and he wrote the solemn little preface to the second edition, he rationalized his purpose into an attempt to reconcile the two worlds which the eighteenth century knew always to exist. He suggested that he had attempted to blend two kinds of romance, 'the ancient and the modern'. In the modern, 'the great resources of fancy have been dammed up, by a strict adherence to common life'. On the other hand, in the old romances, 'the heroes and heroines of ancient days, were as unnatural as the machines employed to put them in motion'.

It has been said that Walpole's favourite materials in the structure of Strawberry Hill were 'lath, plaster and wood', which made his friend George James Williams say of him towards the end of his life 'that he had outlived three sets of his own battlements'.[2] The materials differ little from those of *The Castle of Otranto*. Admirably as it reads as a story, it is a pasteboard structure and one is not a little surprised in the preface to find

[1] 9 March, 1765.
[2] Lord Dover in the introduction to *The Castle of Otranto* (1834).

Walpole using Shakespeare as a comparison in explaining his methods. The emotional life out of which *The Castle of Otranto* had arisen was far stronger than the artistic form in which it gained expression. The eighteenth century in its striving towards a world of romantic imagination is led to antiquarianism, to literary forgery, to the tale of terror, but never to great poetic achievement. Walpole could not have foreseen how numerous the spawn of his gothic story would be, and his intentions were more solid than those of most of his successors. As it is, he remains a person divided against himself, not as the great poets, Chaucer, Spenser and Milton, writing as integrated personalities with a unity of life and literary achievement.

It may seem unnecessary to discuss Walpole in comparison with the great artists, but unless the range of romantic sensibility in the eighteenth century is fully appreciated the work of the so-called 'Romantic Revival' cannot be understood. Scott is the eighteenth-century romantic, with genius added, knowing that 'the literary character with all its duties was perfectly reconcilable with the habits of a man of business and man of the world'.[1] He knew that the practical world existed and valued it, allowing the world of imagination to exist apart, profitably apart, in anonymity. Shelley inherited this dubious eighteenth-century romanticism, this Vathek world, useless for his own purposes, and his story as a poet is his gradual conversion from it into the greater world of Greek mythology. The influence on Byron is even more illuminating; he had the same excess of early sensibility as Beckford, even the family scandal, the rumours, and the wild escapades. Byron, like

[1] R. P. Gillies in *Memoirs of a Literary Veteran*, 1851.

Shelley, had to fight his way through to a reaction against eighteenth-century romanticism, though with him the admiration for Pope helps, with other influences, to evolve the maturity of *Don Juan*. All this is to anticipate, yet if Walpole's preface to *The Castle of Otranto* is read along with his letters it can be seen that he was attempting to create an 'irregular' and romantic literature in opposition to the tradition of Pope which he never fully appreciated. To Élie de Beaumont he wrote with reference to his story: 'How will you be amazed to hear that a country of whose good sense you have an opinion should have applauded so wild a tale! But you must remember, Sir, that whatever good sense we have, we are not yet in any light chained down to precepts and inviolable laws. . . . We still prefer the extravagant beauties of Shakespeare and Milton to the cold and well-disciplined merit of Addison and even to the sober and correct march of Pope.'[1]

The anomaly in the eighteenth century is that while the 'romantic' indulgences for which Walpole stood were so widespread, far more then than in the period of the so-called romantic revival, it was the other side of poetry, 'the sober and correct march' of the couplets, that alone produced the great artists, in Pope first and then in Johnson. Walpole and those who shared his gothic and romantic delights attempt to obscure the picture by suggesting a decline in Pope's reputation. To accept this is again to falsify the whole picture of the age. Pope's work continued in popularity, not from a tyranny of the couplet, which never existed, but for its own sound merits. Walpole, who never assigned Pope an adequate place as a poet, shows an intimate

[1] 18 March, 1765.

THE EIGHTEENTH CENTURY 87

knowledge of his work. Johnson when he came to write his *Life of Pope* was not defending a losing cause, but making a sober analysis of a poet in whom he and a great part of the world of good taste still delighted. Not all Pope's defenders used the bold language of Percival Stockdale: 'Pope is an English Pegasus; adorned with splendid trappings; holding a bold and animated career and disdaining the ground.'[1] Stockdale had a distaste for the 'gothic' and its extravagances; he is a partisan and petulant critic but he was not speaking for himself alone in his ironical attack: 'in painting, let all your figures be grotesque, let all your colouring be Chinese. Give them a huddle, and a crash of objects; the gardens of Sir William Chambers;—the very Advertisements of a Langford: the very Poetry of the Wartons.'

The most sober evidence of Pope's continued popularity comes from the record of editions and of continual references. That popularity remained strong in the early nineteenth century, in the so-called romantic period. J. J. van Rennes, who has devoted an interesting volume[2] to the debate of Bowles and Byron on Pope, speaks of those interested at the time in the controversy as 'a few Pope idolators, a few who still clung to old traditions. . . . The victory of romanticism over classicism was complete; the taste of the reading public was changing'. The evidence is overwhelming against this conclusion. From 1800 to 1830 Pope was read far more than Wordsworth, as the numerous reissues of the *Iliad* and the *Essay on Man* show, apart from the new

[1] *An Enquiry into the Nature and Genuine laws of Poetry*, 1778.
[2] *Bowles, Byron and the Pope-Controversy*, J. J. van Rennes, Amsterdam, 1927.

editions of the collected works. Against Mr. van Rennes there is Wordsworth's own testimony given in his comment on the translation of the moonlight scene in the *Iliad*: 'the verses of Dryden, once highly celebrated are forgotten: those of Pope still retain their hold upon public estimation,—nay, there is not a passage of descriptive poetry, which at this day finds so many and such ardent admirers.'

The only poetry which could compete with Pope in the early nineteenth century was that of Scott and Byron, which was in great part the poetry of those gothic sensibilities which the eighteenth century had felt but had never been able to render poetically. Even the antagonism to Pope among the 'romantic' poets is never as widespread as the histories of literature would have us believe. It centres in Keats who learned it, along with many other things good and bad, from Hazlitt. Shelley is untouched by it, and Coleridge's judgments in the *Biographia Literaria*, though mainly in footnotes, are wise and illuminating. Wordsworth attacked Pope in the *Prefaces* for propaganda purposes but never with the virulence with which he opposed the other side of the eighteenth century—the 'gothic' romances and *Ossian*. His verse shows that he had studied Pope with attention and in his letters he advises one correspondent to read the description of the Cave of Spleen in *The Rape of the Lock*, and on another occasion refers allusively to *Eloisa and Abelard*.

The eighteenth century developed a poetry distinct from that of Pope and from the gothic world of Beckford and Walpole. In 1726 James Thomson published his *Winter*. The poem in its ever-expanding form of *The Seasons* was widely popular in England and gained a

European reputation of long duration. It was read not only by the learned but by those who knew no other poem. One eighteenth-century critic writes: 'I have found it in the hands of Shepherds, in the remotest solitudes, who never saw another book, save their Bible; and heard some of its finest passages repeated by Clowns who had no motive for getting it by heart, but that of delineating so well, many scenes and circumstances, in which they not necessarily are deeply interested.'[1] The history of poetic taste in the eighteenth century will be more clearly understood when it is realized that Pope's audience belonged to one social group and Thomson's largely to another.

Natural description has claims to be one of the oldest features of our poetry, and with description the identification of human moods with nature. To this degree, its introduction in the third decade of the eighteenth century was no novelty. It was present in Anglo-Saxon poetry, in Chaucer, Spenser, and in Shakespeare, particularly in his imagery, while Milton's most extended use had led with some encouragement from Virgil to the rural poetry, for which so many writers of talent in the eighteenth century had a taste. Thomson achieved more than Milton's eighteenth-century imitators, partly because he was a better and more courageous poet, and partly from his awareness of a new direction for poetry. In his preface to the second edition of *Winter* (1726) he claims nature description as the great poetical theme. Much is trivial in 'the wintry World of Letters', and 'nothing can have a better Influence towards the Revival of Poetry than the chusing of great and serious Subjects'.

[1] *Strictures, Critical and Sentimental on Thomson's Seasons*, J. More (London), 1777.

Both ancient and modern poets have delighted in 'the wild romantic Country', and Thomson adds, 'I know no Subject more elevating, more amusing; more ready to awake the poetical Enthusiasm, the philosophical Reflection, and the moral Sentiment than the *Works of Nature.*'

Apart from his own capacities as a poet, which, though high, were obviously not of the first order, Thomson's work has limitations arising directly from its form and choice of subject. For the permanent theme of human actions he had substituted the sentimental and fancied relationship between man and rural life and nature. The poetry which has man at its centre will, despite all differences of social habit and faith, remain intelligible, but nature, as Thomson and others understood it, has now been seen to express only one intermittent relationship in man's life. He was dependent in part on an admiration for the picturesque, for the composed picture, discovered or constructed in the natural scene, popular in his time, and arising from the long belief that poetry and painting were arts which could serve the same descriptive purposes.[1] Poetry that is mere description is poetry that has lost its vitality, as Lessing was later to demonstrate. Poetry that is mere nature description is poetry that has turned away from much civilized man has accumulated out of life.

Thomson seems unaware of the discussions on the meaning of poetry which have preceded him, and yet he is reaching out, somewhat naïvely, to a solution of the difficulties with which earlier poets had found themselves confronted. If neither classical mythology nor Christian

---

[1] *The Picturesque*, Christopher Hussey, 1927.

THE EIGHTEENTH CENTURY

story can provide the motive for a poem, let the description of nature be substituted. This is only to give effect to Dryden's surmise that the introspective poem might, under a Christian system, replace the poem of action. Thomson may not seem acutely introspective in the odd medley which makes up *The Seasons*, yet in the central movement the poet is viewing nature, and so individual feeling is substituted for a general or universal action.

The most definite opposition to Pope came from a group of critics in the middle of the century whose work centres in that of the brothers, Joseph and Thomas Warton. Even critics, such as George Saintsbury, who are given to measured statement, speak of them as 'harbingers of the dawn' of romanticism.[1] The two brothers and those associated with them had new loyalties in verse, which included the Greek ode, Milton's minor poems, and medieval verse. But only in Collins and in Gray did the group produce poets. The main contribution of the two brothers lay in criticism, in literary history and in antiquarianism, and their influence on the development of the art of poetry in England has often been exaggerated. No good purpose can be served by attempting in return to minimize their importance. Thomas Warton first executed a history of English poetry, which whatever its shortcomings, and they are more numerous than the venomous Ritson could detect, first laid the foundations for studying the continuity of our poetry. Warton acknowledged the place of Anglo-Saxon verse, explored, with some detail, medieval poetry, gave a lengthy appraisal of Chaucer and studied Spenser from the background of his English and Italian antece-

[1] *History of Criticism*, Vol. III, p. 53.

dents. Through his scholarship he opened up the ways to that 'gothic' literature in which the eighteenth century became so widely interested. But this he did without ever losing his admiration for the classics or for that world of good sense which neo-classicism had given to the eighteenth century. This is sometimes spoken of as hesitancy and an absence of clear purpose. Rather it indicates Thomas Warton's sound sense and his freedom from any partisan spirit.[1] He is like an eighteenth-century gentleman who has no desire to give up his Palladian residence because there are 'gothic' ruins in the garden; above all he does not wish to live in the ruins. At the close of the second book of his history he contrasts the eighteenth century with the 'gothic' ages, and like so many others at that time he wishes to make the best of both worlds. The gain has been 'much good sense, good taste and good criticism', while 'we have lost a set of manners and a system of machinery, more suitable to the purposes of poetry than those which have been adopted in their place. We have parted with extravagances that are above propriety, with incredibilities that are more acceptable than truth, and with fictions that are more valuable than reality'. Warton's *Verses on Sir Joshua Reynolds's Painted Window at New College, Oxford* (1782), have often been taken as a recantation of his 'gothic' enthusiasms. Actually Warton at any period of his life had admired both 'chaste design' and the 'vaulted dome'.

Joseph Warton's *Essay on the Genius and Writings of Pope* has equally admiration mingled with criticism. This eminently reasonable attitude is assumed by those who, with Saintsbury, see the *Essay* only as a 'document

[1] See *Warton's History of English Poetry*, by D. Nichol Smith, 1929.

in the Romantic Revolt' to be a mixture of uncertainty and cowardice. Saintsbury in a witty but unjust phrase writes that the *Essay* 'almost literally anticipates the jest of a hundred years later on another document, about chalking up "No Popery!" and then running away'.[1]

Warton gives an honest and clear image of his conclusions, and these parallel closely the sense of loss and gain which his brother had found in the comparison of medieval and modern poetry. To write that 'the Time-Spirit is carrying the man along, but he is carried half-unconsciously',[1] seems to lose historical perspective in a desire to construct literary history. Judgment on Warton's *Essay* as a whole is obscured by the fact that it is best remembered in its dedication to Edward Young, and here, possibly for the very reason that he is writing to Young, a greater emphasis comes into Warton's expression. Here he is drawn into the substitution of the terms 'creative imagination' for the more sober classical term 'imitation'. Also he attempts to separate the work of poets into hierarchies with Spenser, Shakespeare and Milton alone in the first order. In the *Essay* he does not run away from the *Dedication* but finds himself forced to qualify it by his intimate and understanding interpretation of Pope's verse. Even in the *Dedication* in his boldest assertions he is only affirming in more enthusiastic language what Horace, or even Pope himself, had written with some change of emphasis. 'A clear head,' he writes, 'and acute understanding are not sufficient alone to make a poet; it is a creative and glowing imagination, "acer spiritus ac vis", and that alone, that can stamp a writer with this exalted and very uncommon character.'

[1] Saintsbury, *History of Criticism*, Vol. III, pp. 66–7.

The Wartons were scholars and antiquarians, and their statements are measured and intelligible. They held a middle course not because they were precursors but because they saw that poetry could fulfil itself in more than one way. Their conclusions may be contrasted with the vaunting claims made in Edward Young's *Conjectures on Original Composition* of 1759. The absence of restraint in this essay is difficult to parallel in our criticism. Young, in defending unrestricted liberty for genius, could exclaim: 'Genius can set us right in Composition without the rules of the learned, as conscience sets us right in life without the laws of the land.' In his passage on 'Originals' he seems to deny the whole strength and virtue of tradition for: 'suppose an Imitator to be the most excellent (and such there are), yet still he but nobly builds on another's foundation: his debt is, at least, equal to his glory; which, therefore, on the balance, cannot be very great. On the contrary, an *Original* though but indifferent (its *Originality* being set aside), yet has something to boast.' All that was valuable and permanent in Young had been conceded by Addison and Pope and Johnson. All that he added was critical enthusiasm and extravagance, strange in so old a man, and accompanied by a fiddling attack on Swift, a sneer at Pope for his Catholicism, and some quotations from Bacon, with a bleak misunderstanding of his attitude to literature. Here was the little Bethel of criticism, deluding itself into a belief in its own apotheosis. Modern writers,[1] in rescuing Young's

[1] See Edith J. Morley, *Edward Young's Conjectures*, 1918: M. W. Steinke, *Edward Young's 'Conjectures' in England and Germany*, New York, 1917: J. L. Kind, *Edward Young in Germany*, New York, 1906: W. Thomas, *Le Poète Edward Young*, 1901.

Conjectures from oblivion, have exaggerated his importance by implying that he had an influence as a critic in England. There is no influence from Young on Wordsworth, or Shelley or Keats, and certainly in no direct way on Coleridge. One of his supporters, W. Steinke, after speaking of Young as part of the 'Romantic Movement', admits that his 'very little influence of the treatise on later English writers can be discovered.'[1] Unless he influenced Joseph Warton in the dedication of the *Essay on Pope*, it is difficult to find that his criticism influenced even his contemporaries. The only writer who speaks the same language as Young is Horace Walpole in the preface to the second edition of *The Castle of Otranto*. Young's influence lies not in England but in Germany where his *Conjectures* were used in that conflict of 'classicism' and 'romanticism' more absolute and theoretical in its form than anything found in England. In England he influences no writer of a magnitude equal to that of Herder, for the good reason that the debate which he tried to arouse with his declamatory over-statement finds its way, among poets of the first order, to other and more moderate conclusions. Indirectly he comes back, modified beyond recognition, through Coleridge's German studies, but his conclusions fail to draw any attention in the romantic period. Coleridge's conception of the Imagination was philosophical, not a declamatory assertion, and Wordsworth has a modesty entirely out of keeping with Young's pretensions. Keats has a respect for tradition, for the great masters, even when he insists on making his own selection from them. If Shelley's early work may read like Young's *Conjectures* put into practice,

[1] M. W. Steinke, loc. cit.

this occurs only before he has worked himself free of the less reputable side of the eighteenth century which as a youth attracted him.

It is difficult to summarize the effect that the Wartons and those associated with them had as far as poetry and other works of imagination are concerned. Clearly they had made the sense of the past of literature more vivid and concrete than ever before, and with Hurd a freedom is claimed for the artist to develop independently. Especially had they opened up medieval poetry for such as could employ it, and if Percy's *Reliques* may be associated with their work, they had offered the ballad as a model for later writers. While the ballad has a wide influence, only one man of a dominating imagination discovered how the sense of the past and of history could be employed creatively. In Sir Walter Scott, though numerous other influences contribute to his development, the Wartons have their most genuine successor. Scott, above all the later romantic writers, represents the antiquarian and gothic elements of the eighteenth century worked out in terms of genius. The emphasis on the past was not without its dangers, for it led to spurious work in *Ossian*, against which Wordsworth reacted, and it entangled Chatterton's boyish genius in forgery. To suggest that the Wartons were responsible for *Ossian* would, of course, be unjust, but if they must be made precursors of anything they lead more towards *Ossian* than to *The Prelude* or *Hyperion* or *Prometheus Unbound*. For *Ossian* in its gloomy grandeur and its reliance on feeling rather than on thought and action is the consummation of a number of eighteenth-century tendencies.

All this stands apart from their contribution to scholarship, but how that scholarship affected the art of poetry itself is more open to question. After the Wartons the interest in poetry becomes increasingly an interest in the past of poetry, and criticism is less concerned with the immediate problem of poetry in the age itself. The work of the scholar and the necessities of the poet are set apart. This danger is resisted by those who are most urgently concerned about poetry, by Coleridge and Arnold and Pater, but the temptation is always there. It can be seen by contrasting the methods and purposes of Thomas Warton with those of Dryden, who is ever employing criticism and such history as is available to further the ends of poetry in his own day.

No period has been subjected to more facile generalizations than the eighteenth century. They usually conform to a pattern, in which the century is described as 'common-sense' and 'classical', with numerous reactions against these standards from the 'precursors' of the 'dawn of romanticism'. Such a summary does injustice to the century itself and to what comes after it. Its achievements in prose, and orderly investigation, and its share in the expansion of England lie outside this immediate inquiry, but within those activities which contribute towards the making of poetry and its discussion, the eighteenth century presents no single purpose, nor principles easily codified, but rather a complexity of multifarious activity. While its most solid achievement poetically, apart from Gray, Collins, and Smart, is in the couplet with Pope and Johnson, there is throughout the century a desire for some satisfaction which this poetry could not give. The whole of that longing may, if it is found convenient, be described as 'romantic', though the term would be difficult to define, and must be kept completely distinct from the purposes of Blake, Wordsworth, Shelley or Keats. It must be remembered that it is an eighteenth-century manifestation, which, while it influences certain later artists of the early nineteenth century, is injurious and hostile to the purposes of most of them. In discussing the 'dawn of romanticism' in the eighteenth century the historians of literature speak of it as a manifestation wholly excellent, very much as the Renaissance is similarly acclaimed. But though much was gained in an increase in the knowledge of early literature, and in the increase of sensibility, there is the other side of the account, the corruption of taste which the gothic tales introduced, and the quest for the morbid to which even the pious Edward Young made his contribution. If English 'romanticism' is to be defined from the achievement of the early nineteenth century, the more carefully the contrasts with the eighteenth century are examined the better.

VII

THOMAS GRAY AND WILLIAM BLAKE

THE term 'romantic', as it has been commonly used in criticism, has been seen to have only limited utility in the discussion of English poetry. Rather it would appear that in England there has been a continuity of tradition, with variations and departures, but without aggressive rejection of what seemed best in the past. Into that tradition elements have entered with changing emphasis to which the term 'romantic' by the definitions already discussed could be applied. There remains a more important contrast, not easily covered by the terms 'romantic' and 'classical', which can be found at the close of the eighteenth century. In its most obvious form it can be seen in the contrast of the work of Gray and Blake. Criticism has often described Gray as a 'pre-romantic', and Blake as a 'complete romantic'; the first term is almost meaningless and the second so diffuse as to be useless if the same expression characterizes the work of Scott and of Keats. The contrast between them is a contrast in the conception of poetry and its function, and this in turn is related to their interpretation of tradition.

Gray is a scholar in the Renaissance manner. For him the golden age is in the past, in the literature of Greece and Rome and Italy. His reading goes far beyond the classics, into medieval and modern times, but the ultimate values and standards are those of his classical reading: when he wishes to praise Froissart he calls him 'the Herodotus of a barbarous age'. With all his admiration and understanding of Shakespeare must be remembered the confession that he would rather have thought of that half-line of Racine's, 'Approchez-vous, Néron', 'than all Mr. Rowe's flowers of eloquence'.

Though he lived in England's century of expansion and was not indifferent to her successes, he existed mentally in a static world, into which the belief in progress had not penetrated. He was a contemporary of Rousseau, but to him Aristotle was more important. Literature he regarded as a part of scholarship, one of his genial studies, with its sources and true foundation in the classics, though with interesting ramifications in the Gothic and Celtic tongues, and with sufficient performance in English to demand a history. He considered poetry, as Pope had done, as an art to be studied, and mastered with that care and revision which Horace had prescribed. He sees the language of poetry, as in the memorable letters to West in 1742, as a continuous tradition inherited and modified by each master: 'The language of the age is never the language of poetry; except among the French, whose verse, where the thought or image does not support it, differs in nothing from prose. Our poetry, on the contrary, has a language peculiar to itself; to which almost everyone that has written, has added something by enriching it with foreign idioms and derivatives.' With the whole of Gray's attitude Blake presents a complete contrast. For him poetry is vision and prophecy, emanating from inspiration. 'The Great Style', he notes in his comments on Reynold's *Discourses*, 'is always Novel or New in all its Operations.' From the past he turns in angry impatience: he will create a system instead of being enslaved by another man's: 'I will not Reason and Compare: my business is to Create.' The methods of Dryden and Pope fill him with contempt, and not their methods alone, for once the early lyrics are completed, and he approaches the Prophetic books, he attempts to render vision as if he were a lonely explorer on a route uncharted and untravelled. Poetry for him is nothing unless it is a new doctrine of life, revolutionary and mystical. The emphasis upon the craft and the tradition of the craft disappear, for the necessary expression arises spontaneously with the vision of a new world. He wrote to Thomas Butts that he composed 'from immediate Dictation twelve or sometimes twenty or thirty lines at a time, without Premeditation & even against my Will: the Time it has taken in writing was that render'd Non Existent, & an immense Poem Exists which seems to be the Labour of a long Life, all produc'd without Labour or Study'. Nor will this vision assimilate itself to any known form of mythology: 'The Greek Muses are daughters of Mnemosyne or Memory, and not of Inspiration or Imagination.' 'Grecian', he adds, is 'Mathematical Form: Gothic is Living Form.'

The criticism of the resulting poems as they appear in the Prophetic Books has seldom, if ever, been detached from opinions of Blake's personality, of his genius as a pictorial artist, or from some attachment to his mystical teaching. As poems the Prophetic Books do not exist, for no one has experienced them as poems. Commentators, it is true, have extracted their meaning, and that meaning can be assimilated, but no one can experience the poems as unities, as one can gain a meaning from *The Prelude* or from *Hyperion*. Some of the poets of the early nineteenth century shared with Blake the belief that the experience to be conveyed was of primary importance in poetry, but they did not follow his way of conveying it. Wordsworth has a unique experience to present, but he converts that experience through poetry into a reality which can be followed. Shelley, superficially his closest successor, has a revolutionary doctrine, but ultimately in *Prometheus Unbound* and *Adonais* he makes it intelligible through the resources of a traditional mythology. It may be that from the point of view of human thought Blake's achievement is greater, though such a conclusion may well be disputed. But such thought is conveyed in pieces, by fretting out a meaning which Blake's isolation has made impossible to receive within the confines of poetic art. In English poetry he has no parallel. The poets of the early nineteenth century, even when their primary purpose is not to express what oft was thought but some original vision, do not forget Gray's method. I am not suggesting that they remember Gray himself, but they rely, with ample modification, upon the method he had maintained, a due regard to that tradition which each great master in the past had inherited and somehow modified. Blake sought an extreme, pitting his own personality not only against the inadequacies of his contemporary world, but against the whole of the inheritance of culture. English poetry did not follow him. I am not suggesting that Blake did not read widely, or that he failed to employ his studies. The influence of *Ossian*, Milton, of Boehme and Lavater, above all that of Emmanuel Swedenborg, are clearly recorded, either in his own notes or in the poems themselves. But he uses them only as fuel for the conflagration which is going on in his mind. He is not prepared to start where the others have left off, for he must make all things anew.

One consequence of Gray's art is that his personality can be detached from his works. His studies, his gentle melancholy, his friendships, and the academic atmosphere in which he lived can all be used to explain the limitations of his output, the form, vocabulary and imagery that he uses, but the poems are self-explanatory, intelligible without reference to the man. With Blake, and with him in an extreme form, this is not true. Before approaching the poetry one has to accept a personality whose experience is unique, and whose doctrine emerging in part from that experience is revolutionary. For instance, one must understand such a view as he expressed in his conversation with Crabb Robinson: 'There is no use in education—I hold it wrong—it is the great Sin—it is eating of the tree of knowledge of good and evil. That was the fault of Plato: he knew of nothing but of the Virtues and Vices and Good and Evil. There is nothing in all that. Everything is good in God's eyes.'[1] This emphasis on the writer's personality, on his doctrine, is apparent in some of the poets of the early nineteenth century; in Wordsworth, in *Tintern Abbey*, in Shelley in *Prometheus Unbound*, and in a different way with Byron. Doctrine, however, can only be judged as doctrine, prophecy as prophecy, and as such they may be valuable even if the attempt to express them poetically

[1] Henry Crabb Robinson, *Books and their Writers*, ed. by Edith J. Morley, 1938, p. 328.

has failed. Any unique human experience is somehow an extension of life, not always desirable if judged socially, but in devious ways an enrichment. It would be idle to deny that Blake brought such a freshness of vision, but it has to be pieced together out of complex fragments of elucidation. In the poets who come after him, and for the reason that they never wholly deny the past even when they insist most as Wordsworth does on his own knowledge, there are poems which are intelligible. The contrast is made clear in a passage[1] by W. P. Ker on Shelley's *Prometheus Unbound*: 'Thus while Godwin's *Political Justice* is a prose prescription for the future reform of the world, Shelley's *Prometheus* is a poetical revelation of the world as it really is in the mind of the poet. It is not talk about Ideas: it is more than allegorical personification. It is reality; active and living beauty made effectual in articulate speech. It is what it represents: the triumph of the spirit over all baseness.' Blake's Prophetic Books are clearly not 'prose prescription', neither are they verse 'made effectual by articulate speech'. They are in varying degrees a mixture, with the failure of articulation arising more often from this refusal to use such elements in the past as are possible for his purpose.

The contrast between Gray and Blake arises in part from the relation of poetry to belief. With Gray no problem of belief arises, for the verse is to be enjoyed as a picture or statue, or a vase elaborately chased and burnished. His verbal baroque, with its memories of older verse skilfully modified, and the long complex stanzas so adroitly controlled, offer enjoyment for those who, unlike Johnson, find pleasure in their rare and

[1] *Form and Style in Poetry*, 1928.

elaborate beauty. Even the *Elegy* with its closer relation to ordinary life demands only sentiment, not faith. Blake, on the other hand, immediately challenges one's conception of the universe, usurping for poetry the place of religion and philosophy. Poetry is not the craft but the experience—he who can Invent can Execute—and the experience is vision denying at once the mechanical view of the universe, and the established religious views. Poetry, as has already appeared, received a challenge of a subtle kind from the new science of the early seventeenth century, and Blake with his insight sees this and expresses in his own way his condemnation of the philosophers whose view of life arose from those studies: '*Bacon*, *Locke*, and *Newton* are the three great teachers of aetheism or of Satan's doctrine.' Nor were the names chosen at random for there are ample signs that Blake studied Bacon sedulously. The eighteenth century had set fancy apart from reason, only to exalt reason, and leave fancy in a world of idle though not always innocuous day-dreaming. Blake, in revenge, would reverse the position: 'You certainly Mistake, when you say that the Visions of Fancy are not to be found in this World. To Me This World is all One continued Vision of Fancy or Imagination.'

Gray's range of interests often obscures the classical loyalty to which he held naturally and unobtrusively. For if his standards are finally classical standards, his antiquarian interests and his taste are prepared to exploit other literatures, and new sensibilities. He was intimate enough with Walpole to be impressed with the more 'gothic' extravagances of the eighteenth century. Even if in the end he doubted the genuineness of Macpherson's *Ossian*, he long believed that they were 'antique' pieces and admired them. At Glamis in 1765 he listened to the Highlanders 'singing Erse-songs all day long'. Much of his interest is an antiquarian one in the reliques of ancient poetry. *The Castle of Otranto* did not affect him as it had affected the author and his one comment is mildly ironical: 'it engages our attention here, makes some of us cry a little, and all in general afraid to go to bed o' nights. We take it for a translation and should believe it to be a true story, if it were not for St. Nicholas.'[1] How small a part in his whole reading this 'gothic' element supplied can be seen from the record of his letters. Never did it disturb his fundamental allegiances, and unlike Walpole, he never wavers in his strong appreciation of English verse in a genuine classical tradition. When Walpole condemns Johnson there is no note of uncertainty in Gray's reply: 'I am sorry to differ from you, but *London* is to me one of those few imitations, that have all the ease and all the spirit of an original.'

He entered fully into that side of the eighteenth century which delighted in wild and mountainous scenery, but this is removed as far as possible from any belief as an education in nature as with Rousseau or Wordsworth. Gray's interest is, in part, an extension of his interest in painting. He is mainly concerned with 'the beauty of the prospect' which may have wildness and terror among its elements, unless, as with Mount Cenis, the horrors are accompanied with 'too much terror to give one time to reflect upon their beauties'. The Grande Chartreuse produces from him the nearest confession that the contemplation of natural scenery may have a moral and religious effect: 'not a precipice,

[1] Dec. 30, 1764. Gray knew that it was not a translation.

not a torrent, not a cliff, but is pregnant with religion and poetry. There are certain scenes that would awe an atheist into belief, without the help of other argument.' But the Grande Chartreuse led him at the same time to read Livy's descriptions of the mountains. When he came later to make the tour of the Lakes the same feelings were aroused in him. In the main, as in his description of Dunmallert, it is the composed picture which attracts him, though again he is willing to be moved by 'the savage, the rude, and the tremendous'. Nor again is his mind ever far away from his reading. When Gowdor Crag arouses in him a sense of apprehension he recalls Dante's *Inferno*:[1]

> Non ragioniam di lor: ma guarda e passa.

As he looks at a view of Borrowdale he is reminded of the print of the scene by Thomas Smith, and discusses from what position the best prospect could be obtained. He travelled the same ground as Wordsworth, but with a different eye, and a different mind. Though with some added vision Gray's approach is that of the eighteenth-century picturesque. He does not even concede the degree of instruction from nature which Thomson had maintained, and it is recorded that of Thomson's poetry he thought meanly. His delight in savage and impressive prospects and in beautifully composed scenes is a widely spread eighteenth-century taste. To speak of it as in any way a preparation for Wordsworth or as pre-romantic, if Wordsworth is to be defined as a romantic, is only to misunderstand Gray and to misjudge Wordsworth. For Wordsworth in all that is most individual in his work is in reaction against

[1] Dante, *Inferno*, III, 51.

the eighteenth-century picturesque. The lakes were a common hunting-ground for the 'prospect'-seekers before he began to write. Wordsworth's poetry described an experience which Gray had never felt, of which probably he would not approve, one which was the denial of the way of life of which his letters are the great memorial.

VIII

WORDSWORTH, COLERIDGE, BYRON AND SCOTT

ONLY when the simple generalizations about the eighteenth century have been abandoned can the varied and, in part, conflicting purposes of poetry in the early nineteenth century be understood. Clearly there was no single 'Romantic Movement', for the poets of that time were themselves aware of different aims, and only a part of their work can be described as 'romantic', whatever definition be attached to the term. Scott in his verse is carrying on that quest of the past which the eighteenth century had begun, just as in his scholarship and antiquarianism he is in the traditions of the Wartons or of Percy. In the novels, of course, he goes further, and Europe, from France to Russia, responds to a new world which memory and imagination have united to create. But as far as verse is concerned he is the eighteenth century continued, just as Abbotsford is Strawberry Hill transferred to Scotland. Byron in his verse tales is little more, though very early he develops, amid these 'gothic' diversities, a respect for the other side of the eighteenth century which allows him to bring back satire from its position as a despised outcast. In this he contrasts with Joseph Warton, Young, Cowley and Wordsworth, who had all spoken meanly of satire.

Coleridge, who has an indebtedness to eighteenth-century medievalism in his poetry, though so much is added, attempts in his criticism to break through the philosophy of the eighteenth century to a new interpretation of the Imagination. Wordsworth is in open and self-confessed revolt against the eighteenth-century 'gothic', and he evolves a poetry which, while owing much to earlier nature poetry, is the record of his own unique experience.

Unfortunately, in this period in which a number of new conceptions of poetry appear, certain poets use a severity in criticism which has not been found previously in our literature. I am not suggesting that earlier poets were incapable of vituperation, for Milton alone would supply sufficient evidence in contradiction, and Pope punished Dunces. But before the nineteenth century the greater poets recognized the masters among their predecessors, and often even among their contemporaries. The two main exponents of this most aggressive method in criticism were Wordsworth and Byron, and their loyalties were opposed.

The prefaces to *Lyrical Ballads* (1798–1804) are the closest approach to a programme ever issued in England by a poet of the first order. Despite their sincerity, and critical value, they are couched in a language calculated to provoke opposition, and they have the appearance of partisanship. The manner of Wordsworth's criticism has often obscured his purposes. These have to be detached from personal grievance and political bias before they can be clearly seen. It has often been assumed that Wordsworth's sole object of condemnation was the poetry and tradition of Pope. That he found himself opposed to Pope need not be denied, yet clearly the major attack is against the contemporary taste for 'frantic novels, sickly and stupid German Tragedies and deluges of idle and extravagant stories in verse'. These, Wordsworth writes, have provided the 'degrading thirst after outrageous stimulation' in the popular poetry of his day. Thus Wordsworth's main enemy, in this first stage of his argument, is not Pope, but that other side of the eighteenth century and its successors, the world of *Vathek*, Walpole, *Ossian* and Monk Lewis, the work which can only be described as pre-romantic if the reference is to Scott, or to the early work of Byron and Shelley. How genuine was Wordsworth's reaction against the wild irregular and romantic side of the eighteenth century can be seen in his poetry. This avoidance of all the excitements of the 'gothic' tales, and of the dilettantism of the landscape-hunting of the eighteenth-century picturesque, remained with him far more consistently than any theory about poetic diction. Wordsworth's antagonism to this literature of violent incident did not present itself to his mind as the opposition of one school of poetry against another, but as a social problem. He foresaw that modern industrial conditions would lead to the 'increasing accumulation of men in cities, where the uniformity of their occupations produces a craving for extraordinary incident'.

Wordsworth and Coleridge found Scott's poetry distasteful for the very reason that it contained these eighteenth-century 'gothic' elements. They felt that Scott was corrupting contemporary taste and debasing the purposes for which poetry should be employed, though their opinions were complicated a little by the geniality of Scott's own personality and his cordial friendship. They cannot express themselves as openly as they might wish, but their letters show clearly enough what they felt. Coleridge in a letter to Wordsworth on *The Lady of the Lake* shows how he realizes the difference between Scott's poetry and that of Wordsworth, and also that Scott is dependent on the 'tale of terror' which began with Walpole. 'Merciful Apollo!' he writes, 'what an easy pace, dost thou jog with thy unspurred yet unpinioned Pegasus,' and then he adds: 'it is time to write a Recipe for Poems of this sort—(I amused myself a day or two ago on reading a Romance in Mrs. Radcliffe's style with making out a scheme, which was to serve for all romances a priori—only varying the proportions)— a Baron or Baroness ignorant of their Birth, and in some dependent situation—Castle-on a Rock—a Sepulchre at some distance from the Rock—Deserted Rooms— Underground Passages—Pictures—a Ghost, so believed— or—a written record—blood on it! A wonderful cut-throat etc. etc. etc. Now, I say, it is time to make out the component parts of the Scottish Minstrelsy— The first Business must be, a vast string of Patronymics, and names of Mountains, Rivers, etc. . . . Secondly all the nomenclature of Gothic architecture, of Heraldry, of Arms, of Hunting and Falconry—these possess the same power of reviving the caput mortuum and rust of old imagery——. Some pathetic moralizing on old times, or anything else, for the head and tail pieces— with a *Bard* (that is absolutely necessary) and Songs of course—For the rest, whatever suits Mrs. Radcliffe, i.e. in the Fable, and the Dramatis Personae will do for the Poem.'[1] Wordsworth's satiric references to *Ossian* show how far he was prepared to go in his attack on eighteenth-century excess, though it is interesting to note that a

[1] *Unpublished Letters*, ed. Griggs, Vol. II, p. 37.

critic of Courthope's discernment speaks of *Ossian* as an influence encouraging Wordsworth to 'romantic sentiments'.[1]

Wordsworth was not alone in this condemnation of these extravagances: he is exceptional only in the remedy he would introduce. Similar attacks appear in a number of minor writers. Francis Hodgson, for instance, in *The Friends*,[2] has an attack, very similar to Wordsworth's, on the taste of the age. Commenting on his own line,

> Adulterate feeling of a German breed

he writes that 'the recollection of everyone will, unfortunately, suggest an ample quantity of plays, poems, and novels' to support this condemnation. Hodgson's remedy is a return to the tradition of Pope: 'it is only within the last twenty or thirty years that those notable discoveries in criticism have been made which have taught our recent versifiers to undervalue this energetic, melodious, and moral poet.'

On the healthy contrast which Pope's poetry makes with the 'Gothic' indulgencies of the eighteenth century, Wordsworth never passes a fair judgment. In his attack on poetic diction he uses a passage from Gray, not from Pope, possibly because it was easier to find in Gray a suitable example. But as the faults of the passage from Gray are to be found, according to Wordsworth, in Johnson, Prior and Cowper and are 'far too common in the best writers both ancient and modern', it is no heavy condemnation of Pope to add his name to the list. It is clear that these defects of diction are distinct from 'gaudiness and inane phraseology' which belong

[1] *History of English Poetry*, Vol. VI, p. 162.
[2] *The Friends*, by Francis Hodgson, 1818.

to the modern writers who have purveyed the 'gothic' excesses. Indeed, in the *Preface of* 1800, Wordsworth has little to reveal of any open attack on Pope. Only in the far more crabbed and unequal *Essay Supplementary* of 1815, when he was affected by his own slow advance to popularity, does he begin a direct assault. Pope is there described as one who sought the arts to please and was seduced by 'an over-love of immediate popularity' to corrupt his own genius. Wordsworth refuses to treat of the moral and satirical poems, which have man as a centre of reference but considers the early nature poetry of Pope as alone worthy of praise. He commends him for 'a passage or two in the *Windsor Forest*', but suggests that 'having wandered from humanity in his Eclogues with boyish inexperience, the praise, which these compositions obtained, tempted him to a belief that Nature was not to be trusted, at least in pastoral Poetry.' He writes Pope down so that he may write Thomson up, and consequently he never allows his own art to come into contact with the sound and intelligible values of Pope's world. His comments on Pope in his observations *Upon Epitaphs*, particularly the charge that 'the thoughts have their nature changed and moulded by the vicious expression in which they are entangled', seems to refer only to the passage which he has under consideration and not to be a general indictment.

Wordsworth's critical methods were unfortunate, for they helped to destroy continuity and tradition at a time when the most urgent need of poetry was their development. As a poet he helped to reconstruct a tradition, but he speaks with another voice, more strident and so often misinformed when he writes as a critic. Byron shared with Wordsworth this same habit for vehement expression in criticism, though with him it is found in a far more aggressive form. In his Continental period, when he has been in contact with Madame de Staël, he systematizes the poetry of the age: 'I perceive that in Germany, as well as in Italy, there is a great struggle about what they call "*Classical*" and "*Romantic*"—terms which were not subjects of classification in England, at least when I left it four or five years ago.'[1] Unlike Wordsworth, he was critical of his own work, and the *English Bards* became in later years 'this foolish lampoon'. At the same time his critical verdicts were apt to be given with a downrightness which made further discussion difficult. By 1817 he had come to the opinion that the whole of contemporary poetry was misconceived: 'Scott, Southey, Wordsworth, Moore, Campbell, I—are all in the wrong, one as much as another—we are upon a wrong revolutionary poetical system.'[2] This sense of misdirection came from a genuine and increasing admiration for the poetry of Pope, combined unfortunately with a fulsome eulogy of Crabbe and Rogers because they had followed in Pope's tradition. 'I took Moore's poems', he writes in the same letter to Murray, 'and my own and some others, and went over them side by side with Pope's, and I was really astonished (I ought not to have been so) and mortified at the ineffable distance in point of sense, harmony, effect, and even *Imagination*, passion, and *Invention*, between the little Queen Anne's man, and us of the Lower Empire.' These opinions in his letters are a more valuable indication of his mind than his long

[1] From a draft of a dedication of *Marino Faliero* to Goethe, with a letter to Murray, 8 October, 1820.
[2] To Murray, 15 September, 1817.

public controversy with William Lisle Bowles, where partisanship is so complexly mingled with conviction. The letters state opinions sincerely held, nor can they be treated as an aberration in a poet, whose creative impulses gain direction from other sources.[1] His great work lies in the satires, and whatever he owed to Pulci, and to other Italian sources, the memory of Pope's achievement, and even Pope's technical methods, were one of his guides. Byron saw clearly that facile verse, such as he and Scott had written in their tales, would lead to a defection in taste, and signs are not wanting that ultimately Scott realized it himself. Again, in tracing Byron's judgments, some allowance must be made for his vehemence of expression and the informality of the letters. To Murray, on 11 September, 1820, he writes: 'What with the Cockneys, and the Lakers, and the *followers* of Scott, and Moore, and Byron, you are in the very uttermost decline and degradation of literature. I can't think of it without all the remorse of a murderer. I wish that Johnson were alive again to crush them!'

The criticism of Byron has been largely the criticism of his personality. The history of his reputation is largely the rise and fall of the popularity of the romantic tales, and of *Childe Harold*. In these poems, as in his personality during those years, he is the living embodiment of many definitions of the romantic, the aggressor, the caliph, fate-haunted, and mysterious, the demon of Newstead, who drank with his myrmidons out of human skulls, le beau milord sans merci, pursued by the memory of secret sin. It was such a Byron who lingered in the memory of many contemporaries, and this was such a

[1] See Ronald Bottrall, *Byron and the Colloquial Tradition*, in *The Criterion*, Jan., 1939.

romantic iconoclast who touched the imagination of Europe. With Byron the personality may be greater than the art, or possibly the art may lie in the expression of personality. But if he is to be judged as a poet, his mature achievement lies elsewhere, in *Don Juan*, and to a less extent in the work preparatory to it. *Childe Harold*, a poem of most varied motives, marks the transition. As Ronald Bottrall has written: 'In *Childe Harold*, in spite of some justification, he is exploiting his imagined wrongs in order to revenge himself on society, in *Don Juan* he is fulfilling himself in a great work of art.'[1] So Byron gives another example of that mixture of forms, which has already been found in Spenser and Milton. If Spenser begins as a poet of classical intentions who ends in writing a romantic poem, Byron who begins as a romantic ends by producing a satire which has kinship with the neo-classical tradition. From the failure to realize that Byron and Wordsworth are following distinct purposes in poetry, or from the greater error of setting the two ways competitively in contrast, Byron is often praised for the passages when he seems to be imitating Wordsworth or Shelley at a distance. So his interpretation of Nature in the third Canto of *Childe Harold*, derived from Wordsworth through Shelley, has often been highly praised. It is not difficult to discover that it is eloquence without deep conviction, and oratory from a borrowed text. It misses the individualized style or the integrity of *Don Juan*, a poem in a method distinct from Wordsworth's, and one of which he could not approve.

Neither Wordsworth nor Byron seems aware of the long debate on poetry which has preceded them. They

[1] Loc. cit.

assert their one-sided and conflicting views without attempting to adjust them to the long tradition of English poetry. The one man in the age who had the knowledge and the critical wisdom to see the problem as a whole was Coleridge. Unfortunately, he was divided against himself. The poetry which he wrote best, and then only for a brief while, was romantic, dream-fashioned, the verses of *Kubla Khan*, *The Ancient Mariner* and *Christabel*. But Coleridge shows clearly in his criticism that this is not what he wished to achieve, and that these poems do not answer to his conception of great poetry. He had too self-regarding a nature openly to expose his own verses, but from numerous passages it is clear that Wordsworth is the kind of poet that Coleridge would have liked to be: 'I think Wordsworth possessed more of the genius of a great philosophic poet than any man I ever knew, or, as I believe, has existed in England since Milton.'[1] Coleridge knew that *The Ancient Mariner* had uniqueness: it might be excelled but it was not 'imitable'.[2] But he knew, too, that it lacked sublimity, failing to effect those purposes which he believed poetry could effect, and in which Wordsworth was to such a large extent successful. When he thinks of sublimity it is a passage from Ezekiel that he calls to mind: 'think of the sublimity, I should rather say the profundity, of that passage in Ezekiel, "Son of man, can these bones live? And I answered, O Lord God, thou knowest." I know nothing like it.'[3] But when Mrs. Barbauld asked him of the moral in *The*

---

[1] *Table Talk*, July 21, 1832.
[2] *Omniana*.
[3] *Table Talk*, May 9, 1830.

Ancient Mariner, he replied[1] by comparing it to *The Arabian Nights'* tale 'of the merchant's sitting down to eat dates by the side of a well, and throwing the shells aside, and lo! a genie starts up, and says he *must* kill the aforesaid merchant *because* one of the date shells had, it seems, put out the eye of the genie's son'.

Coleridge divided thus against himself expended in criticism a genius which seemed designed for creation. He could see the poetry which he was convinced his age should have and yet he could never actually produce it. The nearest approach was in Wordsworth's poetry, and in encouraging Wordsworth he seems more of a poet than in some of his own works. The poet had functions other than those which Scott performed, of amusing 'without requiring any effort of thought, and without exciting any deep emotion.'[2] His functions, according to Coleridge, were wider even than those which Wordsworth had undertaken in *The Prelude*. Late in his life he described the suggestions which he had set forth for *The Prelude*. Wordsworth, he suggested, should 'treat man as man—a subject of eye, ear, touch and taste, in contact with external nature, and informing the senses from the mind, and not compounding a mind out of the senses: then he was to describe the pastoral and other states of society, assuming something of the Juvenalian spirit as he approached the high civilization of cities and towns, and opening a melancholy picture of the present state of degeneracy and vice; thence he was to infer and reveal the proof of, and necessity for, the whole state of man and society being subject to, and illustrative of, a redemptive process in operation, showing how this

[1] *Table Talk*, May 31, 1830.
[2] *Table Talk*, January, 1821.

I

idea reconciled all the anomalies, and promised future glory and restoration'.[1] Coleridge would, therefore, have had the poem more representative of general human experience, than exploratory of an individual experience. He had the desire to unite the method which is ultimately the method of Pope with that of Wordsworth. He shows from a number of references that he realized the difference between 'the objective poetry of the ancients and the subjective mood of the moderns'.[2] Like all poets, he could only perform what it was in them to perform, and his own most successful work, as has been suggested, is far removed from these critical formulae. At the same time, when his mind is most alert, Coleridge is urging a compromise between the exceptional experience of the romantic and the skilful presentation of ordinary experience in the manner of classical poetry.

There are some who still attach little importance to Coleridge's criticism. Sir E. K. Chambers concludes his biography with the comment: 'So Coleridge passed, leaving a handful of golden poems, an emptiness in the heart of a few friends, and a will-o'-the-wisp light for bemused thinkers.'[3] After the work of John Shawcross,[4] I. A. Richards,[5] and D. G. James,[6] it is difficult to understand such a point of view. Coleridge's distinction of 'Fancy' and 'Imagination is now recognized to have validity, and his attack on the association theories of the eighteenth century with his

---

[1] *Table Talk*, 21 July, 1832.
[2] *Table Talk*, 18 August, 1833.
[3] *Coleridge*, Sir E. K. Chambers, 1938.
[4] *Biographia Literaria*, ed. John Shawcross, 1907.
[5] *Coleridge on Imagination*, I. A. Richards, 1934.
[6] *Scepticism and Poetry*, D. G. James, 1937.

description of the mind as an active agent helped to restore poetry to a more important place in human experience. These conclusions have been frequently examined, but a more important consideration remains. Coleridge's theories had little immediate influence either upon poets or critics. Wordsworth listened to him with attention, but there is not much evidence that he understood what he heard, and by the time of the publication of *Biographia Literaria*, Wordsworth was not in the mood to listen much even to the wisest criticism. Shelley, with his genuine philosophical aptitude, assimilated Coleridge's work more easily than any one of that generation. For the rest, Coleridge was too difficult and in many ways too much in advance of his time. It is only within the twentieth century, when psychological studies have helped in the interpretation of his thought, that he has been understood and appreciated. In Coleridge's criticism the poet becomes self-conscious in relation to his art, seeking to analyze within himself how his imagery has developed, or what governs his responses to the experience from which the poem is fashioned. Such a degree of self-knowledge removes part of the interest from the poem itself to the operations of the mind that created it. The poet, once he has eaten of the Fruit of this Tree of Introspective Knowledge, is divided against himself, watching, even interpreting, his own mind as it functions. Ultimately, from Coleridge we derive, in the twentieth century, the increase of an elaborate criticism of poetry in its relations to philosophy and psychology. It has been accompanied by no equal production in poetry itself. Coleridge's influence in this direction arises from the inevitable change which overcomes poetry in relationship to the state of knowledge in general. As has been already suggested, this goes deeper than any distinction of the schools, or contrast of 'romantic' or 'classical'. After Coleridge, the mind has found it difficult not to become an excited audience of its functionings. Such a state is far removed from mental innocence, and it makes many of the older and simpler conceptions of poetry impossible. Coleridge, who sought the unity of experience, served to give the whole of experience this refraction. Not that this affects poetry in the century of his death, but in the twentieth century we have come up to the ghost-haunted figure and had to share the burden of his speculation.

While Coleridge speculated, Wordsworth achieved, and on all reckonings he is the great poet of this period in England, and there has been no successor of equal stature. His problem was a difficult one; it was the same problem as had faced Donne, Milton and Dryden, but with additional difficulties added. In a world where reason was extending its authority, he had to rediscover an imaginative world which would yet interpret life as a whole. His experiences derived from nature led him to develop the solution of Thomson and Cowper, though with such transfiguration that little parallel remains. Later in life he seems aware that the poem of action supported by a mythology would have been a possible alternative.[1] In a note on the *Ode to Lycoris* (1817) Wordsworth wrote: 'No doubt the hacknied and lifeless use into which mythology fell towards the close of the seventeenth century, and which continued through the eighteenth, disgusted the general reader with all allusion to it in modern verse: and though, in

[1] See Douglas Bush, *Mythology and the Romantic Tradition*, 1937.

deference to this disgust, and also in a measure participating in it, I abstained in my earlier writings from all introduction of pagan fable, surely, even in its humble form, it may ally itself with real sentiment, as I can truly affirm it did in the present case.' In the well-known passage in *The Excursion*[1] Wordsworth treated mythology sympathetically. He encouraged the use of myth while only employing it incidentally himself. He wished to present experience without the intrusion of a mythology. To this extent he was in the same position as Thomson, or even Pope, but while they use description and exposition to outline a philosophy or for merely discursive purposes, Wordsworth used it to express a new experience.[2] Wordsworth's approval of mythology and classical legend encouraged Shelley and Keats in their employment, but apart from isolated poems, such as *Laodamia*, Wordsworth attempted the direct narrative, and the record of his own experience. He had the added difficulty that while the experience was highly individual, the circumstances which gave rise to it were often commonplace.

From the first, Wordsworth was divided by a dual purpose. He was conscious of an unusual experience, gained from a contact with nature, and best expressed in *Tintern Abbey* and *The Prelude*. No less than Spenser or Milton, he was anxious to serve society. His unusual experience is distinct from anything in the wild and 'gothic' irregularities of the eighteenth century: it is mystical, with moral consequences, and often closely related to a Christian interpretation of life. Obviously

[1] Bk. IV, l. 717, *et. seq.*
[2] See *Wordsworth and the Locke Tradition*. Basil Willey in *The Seventeenth Century Background*, 1934.

it is influenced by political and philosophical loyalties, above all by Rousseau's attack on the intellect and the exaltation of the primitive. Even when full emphasis has been given to these derivations, Wordsworth's experience remains individual, possibly unique, and his greatest triumph as a poet is that he has been able to render it poetically. Nothing can be more misleading than to suggest that Wordsworth, in this most important aspect of his work, was an outcome of the eighteenth-century picturesque. In a number of important ways he was in reaction against it.[1] The search for natural 'beauties' had begun early in the eighteenth century and became widespread. Gray's letters, covering Wordsworth's own ground in the Wye Valley and in the Lakes, has shown what emotions could be aroused by the grandeur of natural scenes. The ruins of Tintern Abbey had been portrayed as early as 1732 by Samuel Buck for his noble patrons. Lake Windermere had been sufficiently exploited before Wordsworth's poems were known to be an attraction to the readers of the Minerva Press. This can be seen in the title of the *Carpenter's Daughter of Derham Down or Sketches on the Banks of Windermere*, and *The Gentleman's Magazine* comments that 'Windermere' is introduced probably to render the title 'more fascinating'.[2] For the cult of the picturesque, or for the eighteenth-century attraction towards nature, with the exception of portions of Thomson's work, the extraordinary, the grand, the sublime, or the extravagantly gloomy are essential. Wordsworth is no less in reaction against the 'moving

[1] For eighteenth-century nature poetry see *Aspects of Eighteenth-Century Nature Poetry*, 1935, by C. V. Deane.
[2] See the advertisement in *Man as He Is*, 1792.

accident' of the 'gothic' romances than he is against this quest for the exceptional in nature. For him 'the meanest flower', the ordinary scene are sufficient. It is the experience, unique and mystical, derived from these experiences that sets him apart.

The well-known passage in the first book of *The Prelude* shows how anxiously he considered the possibilities of a traditional story for his major work and found the ways closed:

> No little band of yet remembered names
> Whom I, in perfect confidence, might hope
> To summon back from lonesome banishment,
> And make them dwellers in the hearts of men
> Now living, or to live in future years.

This substitution of the exceptional experience of the introspective poet for a general human action is Wordsworth's resolution of the problem which Dryden had discussed. Yet Wordsworth clearly wished his poetry to serve society, not in the way of Pope, but by increasing the imagination and sympathy of men, particularly those in towns. He never lost sight of that aim, though he is frustrated in part from achieving it. From his despondency in 1792 on England's declaration of war with France he recovered only as an individual, but never as an individual who sees his clear relationship and purpose in a community:

> if the emancipation of the world
> Were missed, I should at least secure my own,
> And be in part compensated.

He is moved to unhappiness by the crudity of the new industrial classes. This influence comes too late to affect his poetry, and gains a somewhat unhappy resolution in his mind and in his prose by an allegiance to the older aristocracy, founded partly by personal circumstance, but based on a belief that they could form some bulwark against the moral disintegration of industrial plutocracy.

While the expression of a unique experience occupies much that is best in Wordsworth's poetry, it can be seen from his prose criticism, and from certain of the poems, that one of his major purposes lay elsewhere. He wished to contemplate an ordinary experience, and so express it that it held the imagination. *Lyrical Ballads* contains some unhappy examples, but poems such as *Michael* or *Resolution and Independence* show his success. These poems are completely removed from the difficulties encountered in *Tintern Abbey* or *The Prelude* of the presentation of a keenly individual and mystical experience. In this purpose of presenting ordinary experiences he embarrassed himself with a theory of diction, adapted in part for political reasons, and as Coleridge shows in the *Biographia Literaria* never fully understood by Wordsworth himself, and certainly never followed by him, except in a few of the early experimental poems.

With Wordsworth it is necessary to distinguish different purposes, if justice is to be done to him, or to his place in the tradition of poetry. In the expression of an individual experience his aim is distinct from that of Pope, and from the main tradition of English poetry since the Renaissance. The nearest approach is Blake's attempt to render his vision, but Wordsworth, unlike Blake, can convert vision into an experience which can be followed even by those who have not encountered anything similar in their own lives. To set the methods of Pope and Wordsworth against each other competitively is to destroy them both. It may be well to remember that Pope's is more fully and widely intelligible. The experience which Wordsworth endured is not a common experience, and any comprehension of it is possible only in the very words which he himself employs. Many will deny this, but only because they regard Wordsworth's poetry as an extension of eighteenth-century nature poetry. Whatever Wordsworth derived from Thomson and Cowper, his poetry is a new poetry, new not only as compared with the eighteenth century, but as regards all that has gone before him. Possibly the true inwardness of his experience, though it can be followed, may never be fully understood. Even in *The Prelude* the reader is pursuing rather the individual incidents, though enjoying the added importance and unity which they gain from their position as part of the portrayal of a mind. While Wordsworth is revolutionary in his conception of the experience which the poet is to relate, he remains in these poems, notably *Tintern Abbey* and *The Prelude*, traditional in verse form and to some extent in vocabulary. The resources of Milton, and to a less extent of Thomson and Cowper, are added to his own in evolving a medium. In these poems, and in these alone, Wordsworth fulfils some of the definitions of the romantic. He breaks with tradition in his conception of the poet's material, and yet not aggressively, but from an inward necessity, and in an attempt to solve the dilemma which had engaged poets since Donne. He stresses the individual rather than society, or culture, but while this arises in part from his political antecedents, he seems aware, particularly in *The Excursion*, of some dissatisfaction in his enforced isolation. Nor is this assertion, as in some other conceptions of the romantic, ever alienated from a keen ethical preoccupation, so continuous in English poetry, and it is in complete reaction against the horrors and extravagances of the bizarre world of the eighteenth-century 'gothic'.

Much that is notable in Wordsworth lies outside these poems of an exceptional experience and is untouched by his theories of poetic diction. In *The Ode to Duty, The Character of the Happy Warrior*, in many of the Sonnets, in *Laodamia*, he is continuing, with whatever minor differences, the tradition, present in Pope though with him restricted to satire, of exploring general and wholly intelligible experiences. The application of the term 'romantic' to these, and to many other of his poems, has little meaning. In form and in diction he studies earlier poets, developing from their tradition his own 'individualized' expression, while his themes have reference to the interests and preoccupations of the ordinary man. Their importance may be obscured by their comparative lack of originality as compared with *The Prelude*, but the comparison is unjust, for that more intelligible element in them is their central purpose. They have not the range or the sense of large endeavour of *The Prelude*, and it is by *The Prelude* that Wordsworth must be ultimately judged. Here, as has already been suggested, was a poem of the first order, whose central aim was new, even revolutionary, yet it is typical of our poetry that its fashioning is related in so many ways in diction, and verse form, and the presentation of individual incidents to so much that has preceded it in English poetry.

IX

KEATS

TO many critics, Keats has seemed the clearest example of an English romantic poet. He attacked Pope and the 'classical' school, abandoned the traditional forms of poetry, cultivated a hazardous excess in expression, and, so the account runs, advocated a theory of beauty which excludes any obligation to moral values, or a conception of a social order. Such conclusions are unjust, once his letters, the record of his intentions, are read with the poems, the record of his performance; they are also unjust, though not to an equal extent, in a criticism of the poems themselves. In any judgment, it must be remembered that his course was only half-run, and that the period he had for continuous thinking or production can be counted in months rather than in years. The letters show clearly that he respected tradition as he came to understand it in the great masters who preceded him. The one harsh condemnation was of Pope, and here he was led partly by tutelage to Hazlitt, partly by a realization that if he were to succeed in poetry it could never be in Pope's way. In *Lamia* he shows that he can understand and manipulate the heroic couplet, when he is guided by his independent reading and not by prejudice. Pope apart, he studied sedulously Spenser, Shakespeare, Milton and Wordsworth, and a number of the letters contain his wise conclusions as he tries to keep his own independence while examining the way in which they had approached poetry. Matthew Arnold, who was sufficiently severe in condemning some aspects of his character and his work, found in the end that the only comparison was with Shakespeare. So Keats can be best remembered not as a poet grown stale after his work was completed, but as cut off at the moment of first maturity, as if Shakespeare had died with a few of the earliest comedies as the sole record of his performance.

He had, as Milton before him, a high conception of the function of the poet: 'I am "one that gathers Samphire dreadful trade" the Cliff of Poesy Towers above me.'[1] While studying the past he knew that he had to find out his own way by experience, for poetry must work out its own salvation in a man, and the letters show that he knew his salvation to be incomplete. In the few years which he had to devote to his art he was like the young Shakespeare, intoxicated with words, delighting often extravagantly in their use. This intense attachment to the medium, distinct from that primary emphasis on the experience which the medium is to present, separates him from Wordsworth. He was not attempting to flaunt a novelty of expression, but seeking a language vitally metaphorical, from his study above all of Shakespeare, but of Spenser too and other Elizabethans. His attachment to the methods of his art, along with his patience in revision, has, with however many disguisings, an almost Horatian quality. It led him, in his few years of authorship, from *Endymion* to

[1] All quotations are from *The Letters of John Keats*, ed. by M. B. Forman, 1935.

the *Odes* and to the two versions of *Hyperion*. This self-discipline is far removed from the arrogances of Young's *Conjectures*, or from any of the conceptions of spontaneous composition which have been used to bolster romantic theory. As Douglas Bush has written, Keats was striving to harmonize 'what may, without undue stretching of the terms, be called the Apollonian and the Faustian ideals of poetry.'[1]

The letters show clearly that he did not wish his poetry to be subservient to a philosophy. Despite his admiration for Wordsworth he felt the limitation of having to accept a creed before one could fully possess the verse, and Milton to his mind presented similar difficulties. The superiority of Shakespeare lay for him in his 'negative capability': 'that is, when a man is capable of being in uncertainties, mysteries, doubts, without any irritable reaching after fact and reason—Coleridge, for instance, would let go by a fine isolated verisimilitude caught from the Penetralium of mystery, from being incapable of remaining content with half-knowledge.' At the same time his own verse has become attached to a theory of beauty which was responsible for much in nineteenth-century poetry and criticism. The pre-Raphaelites and Swinburne found justification for their belief of art for its own sake, more directly in Keats than in Gautier or Baudelaire. Keats's exploitation of melodious verse and sensuous phrasing encouraged poets from Tennyson onwards to regard these as the sole objectives of poetical diction. Keats had a wider influence on nineteenth-century romanticism than any other poet of his generation, and it was encouraged by the superficial similarity between his work and Cole-

[1] *Mythology and the Romantic Tradition* (1937).

ridge's *Kubla Khan* and *Christabel*. The interpretation of Keats's intention by nineteenth-century poets, strengthened in some instances by their study of French poetry, led to a separation of poetry from life, which weakened its place in human activity. The influence was unfortunate. Wordsworth could have given them much more had his intentions been closely studied, but with the single exception of Arnold and with him only intermittently, Wordsworth fails to enter effectively as an influence into the work of any major writer. Byron in *Beppo* and *Don Juan* and in his prose criticism laid open before the nineteenth century a way in poetry that would have been a salutary corrective to its own extremes. But while the sentimental Byron is remembered, and while nineteenth-century liberalism creates an idol out of Byron's final episode in Greece, the satirist who looked into the heart and the follies of man is ignored. Keats, to the nineteenth century, presented a dream-phantasy of beauty into which one could retreat from an ugly world. Such a solution is 'romantic' in the worst and most enervating definition of the term. At the same time Keats's own intentions and performance must be distinguished from the facile misinterpretation of the generation which followed him. His own description of his purposes is far different, and, half-finished though it may be, aligns him more closely than is usually allowed with the elements in English poetry which continually recur.

From *Endymion* to the revised *Hyperion* he is engaged in the same problem of discovering what poetry can do. Obviously it can describe or set out the tenets of a faith, or a philosophy, but this is not enough: 'We hate poetry that has a palpable design upon us—and if we do not agree, seems to put its hand in its breeches pocket.'

Poetry, rather, shall be the recollection of moments of beauty. This seems an acceptance of art as a place of pleasant retreat from life, and there is much in the opening passage to *Endymion* to support that view. But the 'Mansions of Life' letter suggests clearly that this self-indulgent, egoistical acceptance of the pleasures of the imagination is only an early stage in the development of an individual: 'we no sooner get into the second Chamber, which I shall call the Chamber of Maiden-Thought, than we become intoxicated with the light and the atmosphere, we see nothing but pleasant wonders, and think of delaying there for ever in delight.' The importance of the significant moments in experience lay not in the pleasure which they gave but in the belief that through them knowledge came. 'O for a Life of Sensations rather than of Thoughts', means rather, 'give one intuitions not consequitive reasoning.' Much in his poetry may seem to deny these conclusions, but the verse is always several stages behind the letters and the letters are the truest criticism of the verse. It is clear from the poems themselves, even if the letters had not existed, that the conventional conception of Keats as one enjoying pictures, and statuary and pleasurable sensations, while regardless of human sorrow, is erroneous. The song of the Nightingale has not only 'charm'd magic casements', but has

>   found a path
> Through the sad heart of Ruth, when, sick for home,
> She stood in tears amid the alien corn.

He began with an intoxication with words, and with an attraction for myth, almost as if he saw the Fauns and Dryads in his Hampstead walks. Wordsworth's analysis of myth in *The Excursion* encouraged him to develop its poetical use, and as in *Endymion* to fashion out an idea in a living way with the half-shadow of an allegory. Thus, he could express his distrust for the mechanical interpretations of the world, the view of Apollonius in *Lamia*, and concentrate upon those intuitions which seemed to give a more certain knowledge: 'I am certain of nothing but the holiness of the Heart's affections and the truth of Imagination—What the imagination seizes as Beauty must be truth—whether it existed before or not—for I have the same Idea of all our Passions as of Love they are all in their sublime, creative of essential Beauty.... The Imagination may be compared to Adam's dream[1]—he awoke and found it truth.' To assert this was not to ignore the distress of life, but to fulfil the clearest purpose of poetry as he then saw it. He is uncertain whether too much fretfulness about humanity may not weaken his character as a poet: 'I have nothing but surmises, from an uncertainty whether Milton's apparently less anxiety for Humanity proceeds from his seeing further or no than Wordsworth.' Such a sentiment would subordinate poetry to a party or a creed, and this was what he suspected in Shelley's poetry when he asked him to 'curb his magnanimity'. He was seeking for the Shakespearian impersonality, the 'negative capability'. The artist must have: '"self-concentration", selfishness, perhaps.' Nor did he wish, as Wordsworth had done, to make a highly individualized experience the theme of his verse: 'every man has his speculations, but every man does not brood and peacock over them till he makes a

[1] *Paradise Lost*, VIII, 460-90.

false coinage and deceives himself.' Wordsworth is the 'egotistical sublime', as contrasted with the impersonality of Shakespeare which possesses 'no character; it enjoys light and shade: it lives in gusto, be it foul or fair, high or low, rich or poor, mean or elevated.'

Keats, himself, did not achieve that Shakespearian character: he does not proceed from *A Midsummer Night's Dream* to *Troilus and Cressida* and *King Lear*. His own passage lies towards *Hyperion*. The problem of whether *Hyperion* is a fragment or a complete poem need not enter here into the argument.[1] It is clear that Keats has moved from the concentration on his own personality so obvious in *Endymion* to a concern for society as a whole. The profusion of detail of the earlier poem is regulated by a design, clearly disciplined and restrained. The delight in Greek mythology now seems accompanied by an admiration for form, not derived by the study of any classical pattern, but developing naturally from an intense study of what poetry should be. The limiting element in *Hyperion* is its acceptance of a creed, the revolutionary belief in progress, the inevitability of a widening purpose in life through change. Keats is never deceived by Godwinian perfectibility, but he is close enough to Leigh Hunt and the radicals to accept 'the grand and gregarious march of intellect' as an axiom of his faith. His modifications of the theory are, however, more significant than his acceptance of it, for he does not turn with anger or contumely upon the past but rather in pathos, for the new order surpasses the old which had in its own time served honestly the purposes of life. Whatever may be the limitations of *Hyperion* its aim is clearly more

[1] I have examined the problem in detail in *Keats* (1934).

profound than those conceptions of Keats's work which gave him the leadership of the romantic and even the decadent schools in the later nineteenth century. It missed the Shakespearian impersonality which he himself praised, and with its revolutionary optimism it lacked that conception of evil that Shakespeare had, and which Pope, when under Swift's influence, amply understood. Its belief in man, as distinct from a distrust in man, is its romantic element when the poem is considered philosophically. Such a philosophical creed is made easier in Keats by the absence of any religious experience. Not that Keats ever mocked at religion, for on the contrary there are ample signs of reading and contemplation on biblical, and even theological themes. It has been said that the romantic creed is distinguished by an absence of a belief in the fall of man, and for Keats, as later for Browning, evil is never positive, dangerous, with every possibility of dominance. Life is rather the continuous development of the better against the good, with Providence as the most powerful ally of the 'mighty and gregarious march of intellect': 'a mighty providence subdues the mightiest Minds to the service of the time being, whether it be in human Knowledge or Religion.'

So far he has come in *Hyperion*, though in *The Fall of Hyperion* he seems to go further in developing his conception of the poet's function. The indulgence in a dream-world present in some of the early poems and so closely associated with his name he sets aside:

> The poet and the dreamer are distinct,
> Diverse, sheer opposite, antipodes.
> The one pours out a balm upon the world,
> The other vexes it.

Success in poetry lies not in the fretful and isolated contemplation of one's own personality as the early Byron had believed, but in the Shakespearian contemplation of the world:

> Thou art a dreaming thing;
> A fever of thyself—think of the Earth.

All this is, of course, a statement of intention, not of poetical achievement. No one can say whether Keats could have carried out the poetical purposes which he was here contemplating. His intellect is leading him to dissatisfaction with what he had achieved, and towards a poem epical in range, universal in sympathy:

> 'None can usurp this height,' returned that shade,
> 'But those to whom the miseries of the world
> Are misery, and will not let them rest.
> All else who find a haven in the world,
> Where they may thoughtless sleep away their days,
> If by a chance into this fame they come,
> Rot on the pavement where thou rotted'st half.'

Much in Keats's verse may offend, just as the Fanny Brawne letters offended Matthew Arnold, by a spurious intensity and a fevered excitability. This can no longer disguise the profound self-criticism and the striving away from unrestrained expression through a knowledge of life and a study of the masters, notably of Shakespeare. Some of his most successful work conforms to the romantic definition of poetry which looks for the far-off dream-like things, *La Belle Dame Sans Merci* or *The Eve of St. Mark*. When he tends to become a philosophical poet, as in *Hyperion*, it is a romantic philosophy, radical and progressive, that he favours. Yet underlying these there are other elements in his work found so consistently in English poetry, a respect for tradition, an avoidance of extremes, and ultimately an ethical preoccupation. They are accompanied by an increasing concern with design, as can be seen in the contrast between *Endymion* and the *Odes* or *Hyperion*.

X

SHELLEY

SHELLEY presents difficulties to the critic unequalled perhaps by any English poet except Blake. To Keats, poetry is his craft, and all his mind goes to its consideration. He is aware that he must also know many other things, but through every activity poetry is the centre of reference. This is no less true of Wordsworth in his most productive years. In another way it is true of Milton, who, though he finds himself called to serve his country as a prose writer, never forgets his self-dedication to poetry. On the other hand, there are writers such as Swift, who compose incidentally but never give verse a prominent place in their own activities, or in those of humanity in general. Shelley seems to belong to neither category. In his famous letter of January, 1819, to Peacock, he writes that he considers poetry 'very subordinate to moral and political science', though in *A Defence of Poetry* he seems to elevate poetry to the highest place in human accomplishment. This dualism is no less apparent in his work. He had a rare lyrical gift, but this he wished to subdue to the expression in poetry of his own creeds. Nor with Shelley can one separate the life in any way from the work. Keats's life in most of its contacts is notable for its sanity, its acceptances of ordinary relationships, and its enjoyment of normal society. Shelley is a personality in revolt, and living out that revolt consistently in his conduct. Judgments on his verse have often been confused by these contrasting elements in his personality. Some defend him unquestioningly, finding in him a rare integrity, and a spiritual conception of life. Others, troubled by his vagaries, revenge the ineffectuality of the angel in their criticism of the poetry. What should be admitted by any unbiased comment is the lyrical power, unsurpassed whatever judgments may be passed on other aspects of the man and his work.

His lyrics were composed in a language whose effects had not previously been found in verse. The intangible and evanescent seem captured in words, through a vocabulary which has an indescribable lightness. It is accompanied by an imagery, often repeated from one poem to another and highly individual, which uses these very insubstantial elements, winds, waters, shadows, dead leaves, and ghostly forms. Some of this spectral quality he may have derived from the gothic tales, though with him that material is made transcendental. His control of lyric stanza allowed him to give these unearthly and shadowy forms a local habitation and a name, but they remained shadows, acceptable to the imagination but eluding the intelligence, from which they fled as if at the bidding of some enchanter. This quality in Shelley's verse is in itself its most obvious romantic element. He can conceive poetry into which the solid elements of earth have not entered, and this quality, sustained only by a genius for the lyric, which gives to his compositions the illusion of spontaneity, is his unparalleled contribution to English verse. Even within his lyrics the duality of his mind appears, for hidden within the apparently airy illusion he had intended to convey some message associated with those social and moral purposes which occupied him through his life unceasingly. The most tantalizing poem is *The Witch of Atlas*, for while seeming at first sight all phantasy, it contains a multitude of allegorical meanings.

Once this praise has been given, it is more difficult to determine Shelley's relation to the tradition of poetry. In his early days he was ready to condemn classical literature, and indeed to turn his back upon the whole of the past, as the corrupt invention of clerics and despots. But after his departure from Oxford his letters are an impressive and almost continuous record of strenuous study. 'I have been reading nothing but Greek and Spanish,' he writes to Peacock in November, 1820, 'Plato and Calderon have been my gods.' His references to his predecessors are few. Unlike Wordsworth he did not attempt to debate his place in English poetry. He has very little comment on the eighteenth century: there is no sign of antagonism, and he showed in *Julian and Maddalo* that he understood the discursive use of the couplet. It is clear that he would have considered Pope's aims inadequate and his philosophy repellent, but he makes no statement of such a conclusion. The other side of the eighteenth century, the 'gothic' stories of horror he knew only too well, and part of his history as a poet is his partial recovery from their influence. In that development he turned naturally to Spenser and Milton, to the Elizabethan drama and the Greeks. The references in *A Defence of Poetry* are mainly to the Greeks, Herodotus, Homer and Plato. He came by 1818 to believe that Homer was greater than Shakespeare 'in the truth and harmony, the sustained grandeur, and satisfying completeness of his images', and further, that 'omitting the comparison of individual minds, which can afford no general inference, how superior was the spirit and system of their poetry to that of any other period'.[1]

In the letters he comments occasionally on literary qualities, and it is significant that he attaches a value to restraint and design. In his letter to Keats of 27 July, 1820, he admires the treasures of *Endymion*, though he suggests that they are 'poured forth with indistinct profusion'. A letter to Peacock of 11 February, 1820, shows that only the more classical *Hyperion* gained his genuine approval: 'his other poems are worth little.' Ariosto, in a letter of 10 July, 1818, he found 'entertaining and graceful, and *sometimes* a poet', but more essential qualities were missing. 'Where,' he asks, 'is the gentle seriousness, the delicate sensibility, the calm and sustained energy, without which true greatness cannot be.'

A Defence of Poetry is more a panegyric than a continuous argument, and its thought as distinct from its glowing rhetoric is often derived from Plato, Sidney, Wordsworth and Coleridge. Its claim for poetry is an extravagant romantic claim, unsupported by examples or substantiated by reason. He accepts Bacon's distinction between judgment and imagination only to solve the dilemma with a triumphant enthronement of the imagination. Poetry turns all things to loveliness;

---

[1] *Manners of the Athenians*, quoted by John Shawcross in *Essay on the Literature, the Arts and the Shelley's Literary and Philosophical Criticism*, 1909.

poetry is divine; it comprehends all science, and is that to which all science must be referred. This sequence of mounting claims culminates in the passionate conclusion: 'Poets are the hierophants of an unapprehended inspiration; the mirrors of the gigantic shadows which futurity casts upon the present; the words which express what they understand not; the trumpets which sing to battle and feel not what they inspire; the influence which is moved not, but moves. Poets are the unacknowledged legislators of the world.' Magnificent, possibly, but untrue! Poetry, whatever interpretation may be given to it, has in no age fulfilled such a comprehensive range of purposes. Knowledge, ethics, religion, and prophecy are all subdued to it. In part the difficulty lies in the fact that Shelley himself had in his life an element of the prophetic; he attempted to live out idealisms which have yet to be fulfilled. He is in danger of confusing the whole of his protest with the elements in it which may possibly be expressed poetically. It must be remembered that in *A Defence* he was answering Peacock's challenging and ironic essay, which had naturally tempted him to speak out vehemently. Whatever the provocation, his own argument soberly considered avoids the real problem of the place of the poet in modern society and thought, by ignoring the difficulties. It contrasts with the continual searching through the same difficulties with the accompaniment of intense thought to be found in Keats's letters. Shelley must not be judged from his prose criticism. The record of his intentions, and their relation to his genuine lyrical quality, can be seen more clearly in the verse, particularly in his development from *Queen Mab*, and *The Revolt of Islam* to *Prometheus Unbound*.

The most interesting thing about *Queen Mab* is Shelley's own recognition of the fact that he has failed. The method is not poetic, for he has only versified his doctrines, and his creed is still the Godwinian which does not assimilate itself to verse easily. How far it is from *Prometheus Unbound* has been well indicated by Douglas Bush, who notes that Shelley in the comments to *Queen Mab* interprets the myth of Prometheus as an allegory of the evils that cooking animal food brought upon mankind.[1] The poem opens in fancy, with the vision of the soul of Ianthe, and in fancy too the poem closes. This, however, is a mere device, a piece of machinery used to start a sermon on metaphysics and politics. Medwin judged soundly when he saw Shelley fighting between imagination and political enthusiasm and driven to convert 'a mere imaginative poem into a systematic attack on the institutions of society'. Shelley's own judgment on the poem can be found in a note written with a copy of the poem sent to a friend in 1817: he admits that it is 'full of those errors which belong to youth as far as imagery and language and a connected plan is concerned,' but that it was 'a sincere overflowing of heart and mind and that at a period when they were most uncorrupted and pure'.

With the realization of his failure he made a second attempt to convey his ideas in *Laon and Cythna*, which was renamed *The Revolt of Islam*. Into that poem there entered two distinct influences: in the first canto, his individual use of symbolism, and in all the rest of the poem the malevolent influence of the 'gothic' romances. The symbols of the first canto, where the poet watches the struggle of a serpent and an eagle, suggest the action

[1] *Mythology and the Romantic Tradition*, 1937.

which follows. It is difficult at first to realize that this fight is not the subject of the poem but a symbol of the great world-struggles between good and evil of which the later part of the poem is to give one illustration. Nor is interpretation made easier by the fact that the eagle represents evil and tyranny while the serpent is goodness and virtue. The serpent and the eagle form some Manichean conception of powers equal in strength, born at the same time and struggling ever for supremacy over man. The first dweller in the world saw them, the eagle was shaped like a blood-red comet, the serpent was then The Morning Star. Shelley suggests that it was in the mind of this first dweller that the real contest took place.

All thoughts within the mind of this first man waged mutual war. The comet was victorious; the star fell: and as the Golden Age ended man 'turned and shed his brother's blood'. Evil had triumphed and its many shapes visited men to torment them. The spirit of Wisdom was turned to a snake, a beast unreconciled to man or animal. Whenever the world rises in civilization or upheaval, the snake rises again from the flood and wages doubtful war with the eagle. So it was when Greece arose; when France broke her chains, or when Laon and Cythna conduct their revolution. In each attack the eagle, or evil, triumphs, but with every onslaught its strength grows weaker, and the snake will finally triumph and Virtue be established.

This attempt at symbolism, though far more imaginative than anything in *Queen Mab*, remains largely a private language. Its meaning, like the meaning of Blake's Prophetic Books, can be discovered, but it lacks the power which a traditional theme revivified through fresh interpretation, will possess. 'The life of reason', writes Santayana, one of Shelley's most generous defenders, 'is a heritage and exists only through tradition. Now the misfortune of revolutionists is that they are disinherited and their folly is that they wish to be disinherited even more than they are.'[1] In *The Revolt of Islam*, Shelley is still welcoming disinheritance, accepting the past only as a blank background on which to throw his own visions.

From *The Revolt of Islam* he moved to *Prometheus Unbound*. In the preface he wrote: 'But it is a mistake to suppose that I dedicate my poetical compositions solely to the direct enforcement of reform, or that I consider them in any degree as containing a reasoned system on the theory of human life. Didactic poetry is my abhorrence.' He had found a traditional mythology which could be shaped into this Morality Play of the human race, following the method which in the *Defence* he had ascribed to Dante and Milton: 'the distorted notions of invisible things which Dante and his rival Milton have idealized, are merely the mask and the mantle in which these great poets walk through eternity enveloped and disguised.' Milton held, of course, a different relation to his narrative, accepting the central theme as historical, whatever additions came from his own invention. Shelley has a simpler relation to his fable, which is a traditional pattern to be modified at will in adjustment with his thought. He was not imitating Æschylus, but employing the clash of two forces which he had found in *Prometheus Bound*, and developing it in his own way. The traditional legend must be adjusted to his own revolutionary creed. In

[1] *Winds of Doctrine*, 1913.

Æschylus he found the suggestion of a reconciliation of Prometheus and Jupiter. 'Had I framed my story on this model,' he writes, 'I should have done no more than have attempted to restore a lost drama of Aeschylus.'

While he has employed a traditional theme, and classical figures, the purpose remains the same as in the early poems, and highly individual. Much of the verse has that evanescent quality which makes exact interpretation difficult. Whatever may be said of the other characters, Prometheus is clearly the human mind, and Jupiter, the Supernatural God, created by man out of man's fear, superstition and hatred. Prometheus's sin is that he has abandoned love for hatred, and that in such a mood he has cursed Jupiter. It is from this hatred that Jupiter derives his power. When Prometheus realizes the error of his hatred, Jupiter is overthrown and Prometheus's marriage with Asia, or the World of Nature, is made possible. Shelley has been influenced by *Paradise Lost* though he has changed Milton's values, finding in Satan the spiritual forces of man and in the enthroned deity the corruptions of power. He has used his reading of Plato for the marriage of Asia and Prometheus, and while Plato's world of Ideas may have replaced the cruder perfectibility of Godwin, the teaching of the *Political Justice* stalks in the poem, however disguised. He has not departed from his early thought, but he has made from it an imaginative life, in one of the great lyrical poems of modern times. This he has achieved not by inventing a new mythology but by revitalizing an old one. The most romantic of the English poets, if judged by many definitions of the term, he reaches here in his mature work, a conclusion closely parallel to the tradition of English poetry. He achieves not the extreme of novelty but strangeness mixed with the familiar, not the anarchic ends that he first sought, but the manipulation of his thought and study in a pattern which, however modified, remains an old one. So in English poetry it has often been: the end is a middle course, sometimes even removed from the intention of the poet as it has first been formulated: so Spenser set out with the pattern of epic and discovered a territory of romance, and Shelley fed with the mixed diet of Godwin and the gothic and ghost-haunted excesses of the 'tale of terror' ended with the pattern of Æschylus. So Milton, with the models of the extended epic in Homer and the brief epic of Job, evolved, almost against his will, a Satan which some later poets were to set beside the 'fatal woman', the Medusa: 'the glassy-eyed, severed human head.' So Keats, who is early infected by dubious models and perfervid enthusiasms, discovers Greece by intuition rather than knowledge and sets *Hyperion* beside *La Belle Dame Sans Merci*, and the grotesque tapestries of *The Eve of St. Mark*. It has been in such a union of opposites, even in the production of poetry opposed to the original intention of the poet's intellect, that the best in our verse has often been produced.

The revival of classical mythology with Shelley and Keats has at the same time its limitation. The classical stories were not native to English but had belonged to a long tradition found in part in medieval literature but consolidated and enlarged in the sixteenth century after the Renaissance. They had entered into the education of Englishmen from the sixteenth century onwards and even if they were not known from Greek and Latin texts the legends were assimilated from humbler sources such as Tooke's *Pantheon*. Already when Shelley and Keats were writing, the audience which found classical legend a natural language of reference was decreasing, and before the century had come to its close this condition was emphasized. With all the strength and ambition which English poetry has derived from the classics there has always been this inevitable weakness that the legends used by poets were derived from another civilization, and other languages, and that once a certain method of education was removed they would cease to be easily intelligible. Keats's career seems superficially to deny this conclusion, but while he had little Latin and less Greek he had a passionate attachment to classical legend, and Lemprière's Dictionary and the Elgin Marbles with his own genius had made more than a substitute for a classical education. A generation later, and the poem which depends on a classical theme is a poem directed to a decreasing audience. From this dilemma English poetry in the nineteenth century found no escape, partly because it failed to realize that the dilemma existed. Arnold in his *Preface* of 1853 suggests a return to the classics without realizing that the world which supported the classical tradition, was largely in disruption.

This, as has already appeared, is the most serious handicap from which English poetry has suffered. With some native mythology its life would have been stronger, and its audience wider. The Arthurian material might have provided what was needed, despite some weaknesses inherent in the legends themselves. From them some combination of popular belief and history might have given the poet a traditional background from which he could develop. But with Spenser as a partial exception, English poets have distrusted the Arthurian stories, and even Tennyson, who uses them when it seems too late, continues to distrust them. The Northern deities, to whom we have some claim, have never acclimatized themselves; they are less part of our national inheritance than the gods of Greece. The truth seems to be that we had to pay a heavy price for the Renaissance, and part of that price was the loss of the possibility that the Christian stories might have developed into great imaginative works. If Langland and the miracle plays, with whatever modifications, had lived on into Dryden's time, we might have found that world where fable and faith unite to provide material for the imagination. The world might have been there which W. B. Yeats desired and created in his own way, a narrower way, out of Irish legend.

Shelley, despite his employment of classical legend, remains the clearest example of the romantic poet in England. Philosophically, he has the romantic belief in the individual, in his infinite capacity for virtue and progress, with the corollary that evil is the result of institutions and despotism. Unlike Wordsworth, he finds no necessity to modify that faith. The spiritual life for him is in the individual experience, as he shows in *Prometheus Unbound,* or in *The Ode to the West Wind,* and though he may create a mythology it is only for the purpose of showing that outside the mind of man the supernatural does not exist. Wordsworth had valued his own experience, but he had found in it ultimately his intuitions of the Divine order. With Shelley the revelation is in the experience, and man's regeneration is not from duty 'stern daughter of the voice of God' but from a trust in his own sensibilities. Nowhere, except in Blake, has a romantic doctrine been expounded so wholeheartedly, and the contrasts between Shelley and Wordsworth are more important than any influence which the younger poet may have derived in early poems such as *Alastor*. That he possessed such a romantic faith can be seen in *Adonais*, where he adapted the traditional form of the pastoral elegy. Milton had used the form in *Lycidas* and nowhere is the contrast between the two poets more clearly shown. They both discuss themselves, but while Milton is consistent and intelligible, Shelley is led away to the vision of the regenerated world which he had already given in *Prometheus Unbound*.

Apart from his philosophy, his language is 'romantic' in a way unparalleled in the poetry of his period. One element in it goes back to the gothic tales of terror, which made such a vivid impression on his mind that they seem to have become at times actual experiences. The images of ghosts, and ruins, and decay, and the occasional melodramatic episodes derive from this source. They are more common in his earlier poems, but they can be found in *Prometheus Unbound* and in *Adonais*. He was recording his own exerience with precision in the *Hymn to Intellectual Beauty* when he wrote:

> While yet a boy, I sought for ghosts, and sped
>   Through many a listening chamber, cave and ruin,
>   And starlight wood, with fearful steps pursuing
> Hopes of high talk with the departed dead.

When Shelley wished to describe the worst tortures of Prometheus his mind went back to those early experiences:

> and shapeless sights come wandering by,
> The ghastly people of the realm of dream.

This derivation from the tales of terror was the least notable feature of his imagery. He developed a use of language not only individual, but almost 'private', though there are no direct parallels. A writer in the *Edinburgh Review*[1] noted one of these peculiarities, without offering any adequate explanation: he noted that in Shelley 'the type is, as it were, transmuted by a poetical analogy like the *hypallage* of the rhetoricians, into the antitype which it originally represented.' For instance—mortality was long ago illustrated by the fall of the foliage in autumn. Virgil's ghosts fleet by like leaves—

> Quam multa in sylvis autumni frigore primo
> Lapsa cadunt folia.

It is the *leaves*, in Shelley, which wander past like troops of ghosts. An example appears in the *Ode to the West Wind*:

> O wild West wind, thou breath of Autumn's being,
> Thou, from whose unseen presence leaves dead
> Are driven, like ghosts from an enchanter fleeing.

The leaves and the ghosts in Shelley are not the incursion of a Virgilian reminiscence, but a personal experience with such a permanent emotive power that it is recorded frequently in his poetry. The association became so

---

[1] Vol. LXIX, 1839, p. 511, *et. seq.*

common with him that it was as simple to speak of leaves as ghosts as of ghosts as leaves. 'Reason', he wrote in the *Defence*, 'respects the differences, and imagination the similitudes of things', but Shelley's similitudes belonged continually to a private world. Francis Thompson, in his essay on Shelley, wrote that 'the sources of his figurative language are specialized, while the sources of Shakespeare's are universal'. The specialization had the added contrast that it arose from the memory of the secret landscape of his mind. So the images of the boat, the stream, the cave, the lamp, and the strange maiden recur from one poem to another. The undergraduate who played with paper boats on the Isis, and who was never happier than when he was sailing, came to attach to the boat, or to the crescent moon which so often seemed its reflection, an associative value that with time developed almost the rigidity of a symbol. So at the close of *Prometheus Unbound* the moon is described by Ione:

> I see a chariot like that thinnest boat,
> In which the Mother of the Months is borne
> By ebbing light into her western cave,
> When she upsprings from interlunar dreams.

This personal imagery, associated as it was so often with intangible and evanescent things, gave to his poetry that appearance of the insubstantial, that strangeness and unearthliness which was so removed from the intelligible theme, or the light of the ordinary world. He was conscious of the difficulty which such figurative language would present to his readers, for when he came in *The*

Cenci, to dramatic writing where the verse must be immediately understood by the audience, he abandoned it: 'I have avoided', he wrote in his preface, 'the introduction of what is commonly called mere poetry, and I imagine there will scarcely be found a detached simile or a single isolated description.' Yet, as Santayana has suggested[1], it would be wrong to consider any of his verses as 'mere fireworks, poetic dust, a sort of *bataille des fleurs* in which we are pelted by a shower of images'! However evanescent or intangible was the medium, Shelley, in all his major work, was guided by a philosophical purpose, and an ethical purpose. W. P. Ker, in writing of Shelley's poetical reasoning,[2] has noted that 'much of it is technical, scientific, philosophical in its origin—like the arguments of Lucretius or Dante—while it never is quite fully worked out as philosophy, and passes quickly into poetical or imaginative modes with forms of expression quite unlike those of scientific argument.' Pope, serving so admirably a world of reason, in a world solid and material, had given poetic expression to

>What oft was thought but ne'er so well expressed.

The final words in Shelley's last note-book[3] are written over two rejected lines for a lyric. They read:

>We feel more than all may see.

[1] *Winds of Doctrine* (1913).
[2] *Form and Style in Poetry* (1928).
[3] *Note Books of Percy Bysche Shelley*, ed. by H. Buxton Forman (Boston), 1911.

They may stand as the text for the verse of one who exploded 'matter—the brute, irrational external world'[1] and following the vision that remained tried to create it through symbols and mythology into a new world.

[1] *Form and Style in Poetry*, (1928).

XI

TENNYSON AND BROWNING

IT is a commonplace in the history of nineteenth-century poetry that the accident of death makes a break about 1830: Keats, Shelley and Byron are dead, and Coleridge and Wordsworth no longer effective. They left a number of purposes which are unfulfilled. Shelley has no genuine successor, nor has Wordsworth, despite his influence on Arnold. For a moment, in *Pauline*, Browning would seem to see Shelley plain, but after that he does not see him at all. Byron, as he appears in the early romantic stories, is popular, but the great and necessary Byron of the satires is ignored. The succession, so far as there is a succession, rests with Coleridge and Keats. With Coleridge the influence derives from the mood of *Kubla Khan*, which is a very small part of Coleridge. The doctrine of his poetic criticism, and his philosophy, fails to affect poets until late in the century, though by others it is not left unheeded. As has already been suggested, Keats's influence is predominant, derived from an awareness of his diction, and from a narrowing and misinterpretation of what was believed to be his aesthetic doctrine. Nor does later nineteenth-century poetry effect that contact with the earlier past which could have strengthened its purposes. Pope, who might have taught valuable lessons, though still read, is not sympathetically studied by any poet of magnitude, and Arnold's crabbed judgments on eighteenth-century verse are generous compared with the comment of some other critics. Nor can one discover any of that intense study of Spenser, or Shakespeare, or Milton, such as made the mental life of Keats so full of interesting exploration.

Some break in the continuity is the first general impression, though in the study of individual writers it needs modification. Criticism has sometimes minimised the difficulties with which the writers of that century were faced. Throughout English verse, from Chaucer onwards, poets can be seen adjusting themselves with increasing difficulty to the changing outlook of their age in its spiritual and social conditions. With the nineteenth century those difficulties multiply. The facile poetry of the romances of Scott and Byron had created a large audience, uncritical in its standards, and unwilling to explore verse which bore the burden of a greater enlightenment or vision. Wordsworth had already seen this danger, and both Byron and Scott seem aware of it, especially when they see the work of their imitators. Bagehot wrote of the effect of this verse with great severity. 'Almost the sole result of the poetry of that time is the harm which it has done. It degraded for a time the whole character of the art.'[1] Poetry itself had created a world hostile to poetical development. Further, the popularity of Scott's novels had diverted the potential audience of poetry largely into an audience of novel readers. This tendency had developed since the middle of the eighteenth century with the popularity of Richardson and Fielding.

[1] *Wordsworth, Tennyson and Browning*, 1864.

Unfortunately, since the growth of prose fiction, verse had produced little in the narrative form, nothing, for instance, comparable with Chaucer's *Troilus and Criseyde*. In the nineteenth century the popularity of prose fiction continued, to the diminution of interest in verse. Tennyson, who attempted in many ways to divert attention back towards poetry of a most profound character, gained one of his more popular successes in *Enoch Arden*, where he accepted the dim and sentimental demands of a vast audience for easy narrative.

These were not the only difficulties. With the industrial prosperity of England in the nineteenth century there developed a society that was antipathetic to poetry. The attack was far more insidious than the incursions of the new science in the seventeenth, for while that was positive and intellectual, this was a bleak hostility of indifference. The increase of urban civilization which Wordsworth had foreseen removed from nature poetry some of its intelligibility, and much of its force as a centre of reference, while the ugliness of the new cities, particularly in industrial centres, tempted the poet to dream—worlds removed from the contemporary life. The weapon which poetry could have wielded in such an age was satire, but throughout the nineteenth century no satirist emerges. Had the classical tradition of the eighteenth century been understood more adequately, or the best that is in Byron, the situation might have been different. Tennyson had sardonic elements in his nature but they seldom escape into his poetry. Too often, as in *Maud* or *Locksley Hall Sixty Years After*, he is content with brooding rather than in developing a clear satiric picture or using the lash of fine raillery. Nor did the criticism of Macaulay and Carlyle, with its depreciation of poetry, assist poets in an age when their task was surpassingly difficult.

The further embarrassment of the poet in the nineteenth century arose from a new adjustment between science and faith, more aggressive than the earlier seventeenth-century debate. In the seventeenth century science had attacked imagination while leaving religion nominally secure. Actually religion had suffered, for whatever were the professions of men their faith filled a less dominating place in their thought. The evolutionary debate in the nineteenth century, while it had no immediate reference to poetry, assailed religion with an open aggressiveness that left the spiritual life of man insecure. The result of that discussion in many minds was a weariness with controversy, which in poetry expressed itself in a retreat to an æsthetic world, a removed Earthly Paradise, out of the reach of contemporary mental strife. For those who were not content with indifference it led, as with Arnold, into a spiritual fretfulness, or in Gerard Manley Hopkins to the development of a poetry which, though it may seem to be reaching back to traditional elements, leaves the poet lonely and isolated with a rarefied medium which he feels compelled to employ.

When criticism detaches commentary on the nineteenth century from prejudice it may appear that Tennyson is its most enduring poet. His metrical accomplishment, as T. S. Eliot has noted, is astonishing: 'Without making the mistake of trying to write Latin verse in English, he knew everything about Latin versification that an English poet could use; and he said of himself that he knew the quantity of the sounds of every English word except perhaps *scissors*.'[1] He accepted the tradition of adorning his diction with as much magnificence and colour as possible, and for this he is condemned by some more modern writers who have attempted the other way of bringing verse closer to prose rhythms and to the illusion at least of a contemporary prose vocabulary. In support of this more modern manner the verse of Donne might be cited, and Byron in his satires, and Wordsworth in criticism, if less seldom in practice. But Tennyson's manner, apart from his own brilliant variations, has also notable antecedents; it is in the tradition of the emblazoned diction which Dante praised, and which in English has Spenser, Shakespeare, Milton and Keats among its adherents. In some of his early poems this diction appears to live in a vacuum, and in a number of the later pieces to be attached to inadequate themes. It cannot be judged by such poems alone, and Tennyson, both in his own lifetime and later has been in danger of condemnation from a concentration of criticism on his least successful work.

He had, as Spenser and Milton before him, a conception of the poet's place in society, which increased after his acceptance of the Laureateship, and his interview with the Queen. It involved him in difficulties when, as in the early *Locksley Hall*, he seems to accept the more facile conceptions of progress, and the virtues of material prosperity. At the same time he was holding the attention of a large audience for verse, the last large audience which read because it wanted to read, that English poetry has had. It was this same sense of obligation which led him to divert his genius from lyric towards narrative, and the long poem, which resulted

[1] In an essay on *In Memoriam* in *Essays Ancient and Modern*, 1936.

among other things in the *Idylls*. Justice has seldom been done to the verbal felicities of those poems, their power of description, and their pathos. Tennyson came, in an age hostile to such a purpose, to treat a body of legend which had often entered into English verse, but had never occupied a great poet. Chaucer had rejected it because it was not sufficiently modern, and Milton because it was untrue. Tennyson would not trust the material itself, but attached to it a contemporary morality which competed with the values of the legends themselves. He was only doing what Spenser had done before him, refusing the temptation to make a dreamworld of romance, and exacting from his poem a moral reference. With the background of the nineteenth century in mind, his resurrected figures are a little wraith-like, as if they moved up and down the countryside avoiding the industrial towns, and the poem has been damaged in design by the moral allegory in a way which the *Faerie Queene* did not suffer. In the *Idylls*, as in so much of his work, he resembles not the poets who precede him but Dryden and Pope. The superficial differences are innumerable, but like Dryden he wished to make 'good numbers', and like Pope his interest was not self-revelation, but the study of man and society, with intrusions into philosophy and morality. Much of his work was not unlike the purposes of *The Essay on Man* except that he had inherited the romantic tradition of vocabulary and legend. Nowhere is that characteristic mixture of influences in English verse more complete.

The early poems show that the temptation to remove his verse to some quiet resting-place away from the world continually presented itself, as in *The Lotus Eaters* and *The Palace of Art*. He resisted that retreat, though he evolved some effective verse in describing the false delights, making the best of both worlds as Spenser did in the Bower of Bliss. While he rejected the more treacherous invitations of romance he never came through to a world of reality, as Chaucer had done in *Troilus and Criseyde*. He had not the gift for narrative or the interest in human emotion, none of that 'negative capability' which Keats had found in Shakespeare. This can be seen in *Ulysses*, one of his most memorable poems. Tennyson himself commented on the poem: 'There is more about myself in *Ulysses* which was written under the sense of loss and all that had gone by, but that still life must be fought out to the end.'[1] The poem is without action, without a character, for Ulysses is the embodiment of the idea of courage rather than a human being. Nor is this courage definite, or practical, but rather an illimitable desire like that of Faust or Tamburlaine, the indefinite yearning which is romantic rather than classical. Tennyson found such an attitude not in Homer but in Dante, and he has elaborated it to bring it into contact with his own mind.

Apart from the exponent of the age, and the moralist, there lay in Tennyson the mystic, fretful and dissatisfied. This can be found in *Locksley Hall* and *Maud* but it is in *In Memoriam* that it gains fullest expression. That poem had superficially the purpose of adjusting faith to contemporary controversy, and discovering a broadminded Christianity triumphant despite the onslaughts of doubt and materialism. Actually it is so much more, and its ultimate result so different. Its many scenes, keenly visualized and conveyed, unite in a

[1] *Memoir*, I, 196.

vocabulary uniquely contrived for this poem to give the vision of a mind, lonely and scared, in a world that has no meaning. The religious conclusion is less impressive than this vision, less convincing, than the frightened child who weeps in the night seeking the comfort of a parent. Superficially the poem expresses the age, but more profoundly goes down beneath the age and exposes it. As a philosophical poem it has no parallel in the nineteenth century in strength, originality, or technical excellence. Of all Tennyson's work it is here that his talent for the short lyric is combined most successfully with his desire to produce a long poem. He has failed to give a poem of action, but in the tradition of *The Prelude* he has given a meditative poem, and if he falls short of Wordsworth in originality he has made a poem more widely intelligible.

Few poets drew so freely both from classical sources and romantic fable, though as sometimes before in English poetry one feels that there might have been some added strength had the classical tradition been stronger. Some of his most successful poems were on classical themes, *Œnone*, *Ulysses*, *Tithonus*, *Lucretius*, *Tiresias*, *Demeter and Persephone*. Apart from these he interested himself in translating fragments from Homer, in experimenting with classical measures, and almost anywhere in his verse the memory of a Virgilian line can enter in. He failed, however, to use mythology in the imaginative ways of Keats or Shelley. Nor did all his classical knowledge stand between him and the composition of *Enoch Arden*. He had not a completely integrated personality as had Milton or Keats; they show some consistent development in relation to the traditions of verse which they study. Tennyson is not one but several, a city divided against itself with his brilliant technique as a diplomatic contact officer. There was the official Tennyson of the Watts portrait and the Inverness Cape who had a sense of responsibility to a vast, popular audience. This was the most vulnerable Tennyson but not to be despised. Distinct from this was the self-tortured mystic whose poem is *In Memoriam*, the greatest of his longer poems. There was a third Tennyson, the satirist who sat in his study, with his pipe dripping over with shag and the port decanter at his side, couching his sardonic remarks. Unfortunately, this Tennyson rarely escaped into the verse.

With all that is meritorious in Tennyson's own work, his poetry gives no promise for the future. In part his own elaboration seems to suggest that poetry cannot well seek further refinements. More subtly one has the sense that the background of culture which English poetry has possessed since the Revival of Learning and the tradition of sentiment which existed since Chaucer, are breaking down. There remains no longer a compact society which a poet can address as with Pope. Nor with Tennyson is there any consistent resistance to the disruptive elements as in Wordsworth or Shelley. Much of his poetry lingers over the past, not with the hope that it can be used again in some new, imaginative way but with the sense that it is seen now for a last time before it is lost. The change in the face of England, and the grim materialism of the new plutocracy, affect him even when he is least aware of their influence. It is this which ultimately makes him distrust the Arthurian material as a mid-nineteenth-century theme. The more poignant passages of *In Memoriam* confess his loneliness, even his despair, but while this is his truest expression he answered his age in so many other moods, and so skilfully, that the ultimate impression is uncertain.

The novel had captured narrative from poetry and Tennyson made no successful attempt to win it back again. It has never been won back successfully, for prose has all the advantages in dialogue and description. Tennyson's work, and much that follows his in the nineteenth century, would suggest that poetry must now make itself as much unlike prose as possible, attempting 'a poem in which the purely poetic genius declares itself most truly as distinct from all other kinds of genius.'[1] Yet Tennyson's contemporary, Browning, based much of his verse on the assumption that whatever prose might do, verse could do also. His early dramatic monologues develop into *The Ring and the Book*, which Henry James thought of as a prose novel. Superficially Browning is a realist, interested in men and women, and returning as some of his more ardent admirers would suggest to the tradition of Shakespeare. Yet one has not to proceed very far to see that Browning's world has little in common with that 'negative capability' which Keats admired in Shakespeare, nor did he ever emulate that imaginative transmutation of language which brings the poet in Shakespeare into equality with Shakespeare the dramatist.

Browning, even more than Tennyson, suggests that a long order of tradition is breaking down. He had, of course, a wide interest in classical literature,[2] but that enters only incidentally and never as an effective control

---

[1] W. P. Ker in *Form and Style*, 1928.
[2] A much explored subject as R. Spindler's *Robert Browning und die Antike* (Leipsiz), 1930, suggests.

upon his design. Nor did he seem aware of the work of his predecessors, apart from the ineffective and superficial influence of Shelley on his thought. Deliberately, and aggressively, he denies the ways in which poetry has been previously conceived, effecting what Bagehot so admirably defined in his description of 'grotesque art'. It has been suggested that he was influenced by Donne's example, and certainly he knew Donne in an age that had neglected him.[1] Donne, however, can be seen clearly in relation to the whole thought of his own age and of the past. Some of his wilfulness arises from his individual reaction to that background. Browning's excesses are committed in a world which he has made up for himself, which, however realistic it may appear, is self-selected, arbitrary, and to some extent unreal.

To say this is not to deny Browning's qualities. He had depicted incidents and characters as varied as those of Balzac or Dickens, but his invention is not definitely poetical, nor does the memory of it remain from the verse in which it is contained. The verse obviously forms an interesting contrast to that of Keats or Tennyson, and to many it gives a welcome relief from their manner. It holds the mind often not from any poetical qualities, but from the effort that it requires, as the eyes are strained to attention before an ill-focused picture on a screen. When the meaning has been gained, the virtues of the language fall away, as unnecessary and discarded. The sane effect occurs sometimes in Chapman's verse. It is different with Shakespeare or Donne, where the satisfaction in the language increases as comprehension increases. The distinction between Shakespeare and Browning is between a uniqueness of

[1] *Browning*, by F. R. G. Duckworth, 1931.

expression and a mannerism, based mainly on grammatical devices. As a result, Browning has no distinctive diction, no recognizable remaking of language. Strange as it may seem, this manner is to some extent natural to him, but not wholly so. He cultivated it as in *Sordello*, and though he may appear indifferent to criticism this excess of difficulty is with him and with some later writers part of an attempt to attract attention, in an age when the traditional might be neglected.

He attached a philosophy to his presentation of characters. This separates him from Chaucer or Shakespeare, or even from Wordsworth. Wordsworth is recording a vision, and Browning so often is only illustrating an argument. The philosophy had the same excessive elements in it as the diction. He inherited the romantic conception of sentiment, and elaborated it into a theory of love which has only its own triumphant assertions to support it. He conceived a belief, which he would probably have defined as Christian, of an eternal life as a perfection of the imperfect forms of this world. Strife and endeavour were the ways leading to that perfection and evil only a half-shadow in the path. This is little different from that quest for indefinite experience and power which has often characterized the romantic, with the addition of a moral and religious milieu. Browning's Palace of Art, and his Ivory Tower and his Earthly Paradise are his *Men and Women*, for they are not real, nor do they live and suffer as men and women who know life and suffering, but as part of his own exuberant theory about the life which he refuses to live. Had he known life with the intimacy which his poems suggest he would not have treated evil so lightly, nor would his optimism have been so profound.

The Ring and the Book brings out all that was in him, and, whatever may be said, it remains a poem that holds the mind closely. No one will deny to it a certain greatness, at least among the poems of that century. But it falls short of Chaucer's *Troilus and Criseyde*, or *Paradise Lost* or *Hyperion*, and in the first place because the theme is not a great theme but 'an Old Bailey story', chosen aggressively because it was that and nothing more. Browning's power over the detail can be allowed again, though often even in the poem itself the detail is left at a level not more impressive than the level of prose. The claim that the story is a transcript of life cannot be wholly maintained, as a comparison with the originals shows, and the modifications have all been made not to bring out a more clearly designed human action but for the sake of a theory which culminates in the Pope's monologue. Conceive of the narrative as a drama, or compare it with some of Shakespeare's 'dark comedies', and its falsities become apparent. In Guido it has that quest for the abnormal which is part of Browning's more dubious romantic sensibility, though with him it is an abnormality that can never triumph, even in this world, for long, and whose workings he can watch with a sense of personal security. The love of Pompilia and Caponsacchi becomes an expression of that ideal which Browning often expounded. All the limitations of the poem arise from a personality that sets itself apart, unwilling to derive from the past, or to construct its own work on the experience of great predecessors. While so much of his work is the emanation of his own personality, he does not introduce himself directly into his own verse. Here he differs from Wordsworth and Keats. This is not because his verse has a classical impersonality but because his Men and Women are a masquerade of realism with which he hides his own individuality.

Beauty, as an ideal, he did not attempt to bring often into his poems. It existed, but in Heaven, and the purpose of his work was to show the striving towards the ideal, especially in places commonly thought ugly and hopeless. Douglas Bush has aptly quoted[1] Ruskin's famous chapter on 'The Nature of Gothic' as an illustration of Browning's theory: 'The Greek sculptor could neither bear to confess his own feebleness, nor to tell the faults of the forms that he portrayed. But the Christian workman, believing that all is finally to work together for good, freely confesses both, and neither seeks to disguise his own roughness of work nor his subject's roughness of make.'[2] With Browning the intention is far more radical. He cultivates evil with the same strenuousness as did Byron, but only that he may exercise upon it the exorcism of his faith. The vocabulary and verse have frequently the abrupt, broken effects which suggest the abnormality of the experience portrayed. The aim certainly is seldom, if ever, towards the resources of language for effects which are in themselves pleasurable.

In writing thus of Browning I am troubled by the thought that much has been missed in my account and that he is greater than these conclusions. Probably this is true, for I can recall pleasures, very strong and varied, from reading his work, such as that memorable picture of Renaissance Italy made clear in a single poem in *The Bishop Orders his Tomb*. Yet here in reviewing

[1] *Mythology and the Romantic Tradition*, 1937.
[2] *The Stones of Venice*, 1851–3.

him in the whole course of English poetry I see more clearly than before a break of tradition in his work, and equally little promise for the future. If he was to be a philosopher in verse he would have done well to know his own age more fully. Italy, though he seems to people it with so many living people, was a retreat from a world he never faced. Tennyson attempted to face it, as *In Memoriam* shows, and two poets in the same age can seldom have been so different; Tennyson with the sadness of vision, and Browning jubilant because he has never seen. Had he known tragedy instead only of theory he might have been successful in dramatic poetry towards which his talent extends. As it is, the distance between *Lear* and *Paracelsus* or *The Ring and the Book* is the difference between the word that is made flesh and the word that is made theory. The difficulty in approaching his work is that so many false responses can be aroused by it, and that even Browning did not condemn them. All the texts are there for the popular preacher and all the illustrations. Part of that falsity arrives from Browning's own uncertainty about the standards of his art, or of the art of those who preceded him. Even if this estimate is too severe, it still remains true that the central problems which the great artists since Spenser have discussed, and the intentions on which their work seems based, seem no longer applicable to him, or sometimes seem not even to have interested him.

He has had a wider influence on later poetry than Tennyson, but this has arisen not from any poetical principle, but out of his mannerisms. His cult of the grotesque, frequently of the deliberately ugly, has given a dubious lead to modern poets who, finding their own world hideous and disharmonious, feel that their poetry should be made uncouth in response to it. He has profited in the reaction against Tennyson, though the way of Tennyson cannot be permanently ignored if the art of poetry is to survive. For whatever his own shortcomings, Tennyson believed, as so many English poets before him, that verse should be fashioned into forms that were pleasurable. The argument that Donne and Shakespeare departed from such purposes ignores a part of their work and emphasizes and isolates other elements which have proved acceptable for modern imitation. If some vision of the world's distress led to the cankered epithets of *Troilus and Cressida*, they were accompanied by images that were full of beauty, and with Donne, even among the cere-cloths the memory of past loveliness is not forgotten. With them the cruelty of life is the contrast of brutality with beauty, and the images of that beauty never lose their place. If life is all bestial, there is nothing worth recording. Browning himself is not affected by this problem, for he had his own balm for evil, but some who have been influenced by him have used his verbal eccentricities to reduce life to a dull record from which every memory of magnificence has departed.

XII

MATTHEW ARNOLD AND THE LATER NINETEENTH CENTURY

IN his *Preface* to his *Poems* (1853) Matthew Arnold makes a bold attempt to bring poetry back to a classical allegiance. He rejects its increasing introspection with the emphasis of an isolated individual experience rather than upon the general. Further, he asserts, with Aristotelian echo, that the eternal objects of poetry are 'human actions; possessing an inherent interest in themselves, and which are to be communicated in an interesting manner by the art of the Poet'. The poet will find that 'excellent actions' are those 'which most powerfully appeal to the great primary human affections: to those elementary feelings which subsist permanently in the race, and which are independent of time'. Seldom has English criticism spoken with an accent so clear, or made so undivided a plea for a classical practice in verse. The results of the *Preface* are informative and unexpected. It had no effect, not even on Arnold himself. *Merope*, and *Sohrab and Rustum* certainly exist, but rather as lecture-room models for illustrating the theory. They cannot be compared as verse with *Empedocles on Etna*—temporarily sacrificed for the principles of 1853—or with the shorter poems *The Strayed Reveller*, *The Forsaken Merman* and *Dover Beach*. His genuine verse contemplated his own spiritual distress, the shadow of doubt which tormented him and which, try as he would, he could not overcome. Its record runs through his poetry, from *Resignation* to the end, and is itself converted into a poetical reality in such poems as *The Scholar Gipsy* and *Thyrsis*. Arnold cannot remove Empedocles permanently from his poetry, for he is Empedocles. In the *Preface* he had condemned those who make their own lives a theme for verse. But a man's poetry will not always follow where his intellect would lead it, and Arnold remains in his best verse self-contemplative rather than the maker of excellent actions. Nor was this all, for in his verse, as in *The Forsaken Merman*, there comes that longing for 'a red gold throne', an imaginative world away from the problems of his age.

Arnold's *Preface* of 1853 attempted to restore design to poetry when the discursive and the grotesque, *The Excursion* and Browning's tradition, were in danger of obscuring it. In its place in the mid-nineteenth century his plea is a marked recovery of critical values, in the same way as his insistence on the high purpose of poetry should have swept away all the spurious and facile verse which encumbers those decades. At the same time the limitation of his profession of poetical faith is significant. Despite his own denial, he was attempting to restore poetry by a return to classical mythology. He seems unaware of the seventeenth-century debate on that matter, nor does he do justice to the success of Shelley and Keats in recovering mythology for the imagination after the seventeenth-century dilemma. In his own age any return to classical mythology had been made increasingly difficult by the break in a tradition of education which had existed from the Renaissance onwards. The classical attitude which Arnold advocated could be achieved not by a mechanical return to the methods of the ancients but by a more intimate understanding of the tradition of English poetry itself. With all that Arnold achieves in the restoration of criticism, in his assessment of the English tradition he is limited. While he can administer censures to the early nineteenth-century writers many of his judgments are caught up in the fascination which their work exercised upon him.

Outstanding is his depreciation of that clear, disciplined work in the couplet which centred in Pope. Arnold can commit himself to such expressions as 'genuine poets like Milton and Gray—artificial poets like Pope'.[1] Arnold in 1880 found the poetry of Dryden and Pope gaining in popularity among the younger generation and he made an assault against it.[2] Yet even considered in its narrowest form as satire it would have been a salutary corrective to the verse of that period. W. P. Ker, despite his admiration for Arnold, was aroused by these judgments on the eighteenth century: 'let me say with the greatest respect for Matthew Arnold that his description of Dryden and Pope as "classics of our prose" is a double sin in criticism, because it confuses the kinds in two ways; ignoring their poetry and their prose alike. For of course they were classics of our prose, when they write prose.' Arnold would appear to ignore the healthy function of

---

[1] *Preface* to Johnson's *Lives of the Poets*.

[2] In the introduction to T. H. Ward's *The English Poets* (1880): I have not traced the special revival of an interest in Dryden and Pope to which Arnold refers.

poetry as satire, for he writes his essay on Byron as if *Don Juan* did not exist, though how different the middle nineteenth century might have been had a second *Don Juan* erupted into the middle of it! His only genuine tribute to satire, and a surprising one, is to the 'superb poetic success' of *The Jolly Beggars*. While he demanded from poetry 'excellent actions' his references to Chaucer are confined to generalizations about 'liquid diction', and the charm of a passage from *The Prioress's Tale*. To the 'excellent action' of *Troilus and Criseyde*, fulfilling in so many ways the purposes that he looked for in classical poetry, he has not even a bare reference. It is symptomatic that in his introduction to English poetry he passes by Donne and the 'metaphysical' poets as if they had never existed. His mind when it seeks for examples goes back to the romantic poets, and from them, since they fail to satisfy him, he escapes, with a glance at Milton, to Greece and Rome. Frequently he acknowledges the greatness of Shakespeare, but he gives no clear indication that he would have advocated any revival of a genuine verse drama. Had Arnold relied less on the calm security of classical literature and realized more the living sense of the English tradition he might have achieved more in restoring poetry to those high purposes of which he considered it capable.

More clearly than any poet of his age Arnold saw the relation of poetry to society, and that his own age was inimical to the poet. In the most spirited of all his essays he wrote: 'The grand work of literary genius is a work of synthesis and exposition, not of analysis and discovery; its gift lies in the faculty of being happily inspired by a certain intellectual and spiritual atmosphere, by a certain order of ideas, when it finds itself in them;

of dealing divinely with these ideas, presenting them in the most effective and attractive combinations—making beautiful works with them, in short.'[1] He realized that his own age did not supply such an atmosphere. He is on more certain ground here than when he attempts to make poetry take the place of religion, leading it to the empty altar so that one can still have the delights of worship without being committed to any faith. 'As the Catholic architecture, so the Catholic worship is likely to survive and prevail, long after the intellectual childishness of Catholic dogma, and the political and social mischiefs of the Roman system, have tired out men's patience with them. Catholic worship is likely, however modified, to survive as the general worship of Christians, because it is the worship which, in a sphere where poetry is permissible and natural, unites the most of the elements of poetry.'[2] Arnold seems to suggest that mankind can live on spiritual capital paid-up by previous generations, but it is less clear what happens when that capital is exhausted.

Arnold's references to religion and belief show how unreal is the classicism he advocated. Had he possessed instead of that allegiance to Greek and Roman models a conception of order, decorum, and obedience, he would not have turned out the Church so casually to set up verse in its place. His difficulty lay largely in failing to realize that poetry can accomplish a number of distinct things, all valuable, and that not much is gained by setting them in an order of merit. The poet may see

---

[1] *Function of Criticism at the Present Time*, in *Essays in Criticism, First Series*, 1865.

[2] *God and the Bible*, and see the well-known opening passage in his introduction to T. H. Ward's *English Poets*, 1880.

as his purpose the portrayal of man in society, or under a divine governance, as Chaucer in *Troilus and Criseyde* and Langland in *Piers Plowman*. Neither attempts to replace morality or religion, though they must rely upon the existence of such orders. Shakespeare equally portrays human actions with the implied background of a world, in which moral and religious values exist. The success of the poet lies in the degree to which he makes a successful poetical experience. His method may be satire, or narrative, or drama. At the other extreme lies the desire, often described as 'romantic', of creating a new order through poetry, either by vision or prophecy or by mere persuasion. Not of imitating life, but of creating experience which some future generation will find more worthy of imitation. Of this, Blake is the extreme example in England, unparalleled and with no followers, while Shelley in a much modified way held this as a purpose of poetry. Shelley advocates such an end for poetry in the *Defence*, though again the poetical judgment on such a poem as *Prometheus Unbound* will be found in its value, not as theory or argument, but as poetical experience. Arnold never distinguishes between these two intentions, the desire to represent and the desire to create; the most fundamental in our poetry. Clearly all poetry is not confined to these two purposes. The poet may make a beautiful poem, as some sculptors make statues, without any reference to philosophy or religion: the tune, the pattern of words, the sentiment, are here supreme, the 'airs' of Campion, Jonson's *Salathiel Pavy*, Drayton's *Nymphidia*, or '*Full fathom five*'. Poetry can approach to music, with a decreasing relation of consecutive thought, or meaning. Here it exists as it were disembodied, the living essence.

Whatever else it may take to itself, whether imitation or prophecy, it cannot depart successfully from this living essence. It must be judged as an experience, made possible by this ultimate quality; as A. E. Housman has written: 'poetry is not the thing said but a way of saying it.'

The poet may be dissatisfied with the social or spiritual order in which he finds himself, and still be affected by it. He can turn, as Byron did, to satire or, as Tennyson in *In Memoriam*, to mysticism. He may also reject his world, and construct some Palace of Art, or Ivory Tower for his own delectation. Arnold had had a glimpse of that temptation and it grows as the nineteenth century proceeds. The poet has, of course, often welcomed such a retreat but for different motives. It exists in the world of delight of *A Midsummer Night's Dream*, while even in the tragedy of *Romeo and Juliet* it is allowed to appear for a moment in Mercutio's Queen Mab speech. For Addison it finds a place in contrast to the world of reason and the increasing mechanical conception of the universe. Part of the triumph of *The Rape of the Lock* is Pope's union of such phantasy with the portrait of his own age. With the nineteenth century the outlook changes, for here the distrust of contemporary life, of the false values of society, the ugliness of industrial development, and the aridness of the debate on religion and evolution when both sides seem governed by a bleak materialism, leads a number of poets to give a sad farewell to their times and to retreat into a world of beauty of whose limitations they themselves are only too conscious.

Such a deliberate retreat is not found in English verse before the nineteenth century, and if romanticism is to be used as a term to describe that movement, it should be remembered that it is only to later nineteenth-century verse that it can be so applied. The contemporary critics of romanticism have assumed that this verse is a direct inheritance from the early nineteenth century, the so-called romantic revival. They have attached large areas of poetry, instead of isolating this movement which belongs to a much more restricted field. Wordsworth and Shelley, and Byron ultimately, in different ways have ethical preoccupations, or the desire to present an experience or vision which interprets life, or suggests a new way of life. They, like their predecessors, find for the poet a relationship with the knowledge and the society of their time. Keats, as has been seen, was searching out for a similar solution. Swinburne, and the Pre-Raphaelites have changed their ground. The influences are clearer in Swinburne, with his admiration for Gautier and Baudelaire, and with his own misinterpretation of Keats. They appear more blatantly in Morris's early poetry with his praise of the 'idle singer of an empty day'. In Rossetti a complete rejection of contemporary circumstance, and of contemporary obligation has been reached. Even the past is only a dreamland through which he can move to select his own phantasies. In his note *Ave* he writes: 'this hymn was written as a prologue to a series of designs. Art still identifies itself with all faiths for her own purposes.'

All three poets used both romantic and classical themes, but wherever the theme originates it is brought within the orbit of their romantic outlook and their romantic diction. In viewing their poetry one must record a declension from the tradition to which English poetry at its best has attained. Once Swinburne, or

Rossetti, or Morris is compared with Chaucer or Spenser, or Pope, or Wordsworth, or Keats, it can be seen that their interpretation of the poet's plan and function has fallen. It can be seen in part from their acceptance of a poetic diction which Keats and Tennyson had made commonplace, the melodious and decorative use of language, with cohorts of magnificent words ever ready for employment. They all add to that tradition, which in Swinburne leads to a language, devastating and intoxicating in its brilliance, but preluding the end of the road. *Poems and Ballads* (1866) carried verse to the limits of verbal music and stanzaic ingenuity. All that followed would have to be imitative or dim, unless verse could work out its own salvation in some other way.

In so relating this verse to the tradition of poetry as a whole, one is in danger of entering some general condemnation. To do so would be both unfortunate and false. So much in Swinburne is like the poem of *Itylus*, a legend transfigured, and full of memories as inexhaustible as those of *Lycidas*, while Rossetti in many of the lyrics and the sonnets has a dim, Dantesque world of vision which can be accepted as a poetical experience. Nor need the quality of Morris's early work in *The Defence of Guenevere* be minimized. These poems have been enjoyed, and may be enjoyed again more than is possible at the present time. Art abhors the lithograph, and the verse in the manner of the Pre-Raphaelites has been mechanically reproduced. Even without the imitators it had within it the source of its own weakness, the reliance on a beauty over-garnished, show-pieces fashioned out in rich colours that contrasted with the ugly world around them. Nor do Swinburne and

Morris remain satisfied with the world of limited beauty which they have created. Swinburne retracts in *Songs before Sunrise*, and Morris in a more practical way with his socialism. Unfortunately, with neither poet did the revised attitude lead to anything that was poetically interesting. English romantic decadence in the nineteenth century, of which Swinburne is the clearest example, does not reach the excesses of the parallel movements in France. This is demonstrated in Mario Praz's brilliant volume *The Romantic Agony*.[1] Compared with Baudelaire the verse of Swinburne seems amateurish in its exploration of evil, half-serious, despite the maze of words. There is no English parallel for Pétrus Borel or Joséphin Péladan. The moral issue is always waiting to entangle Swinburne. Even here the absence of extremes, which has earlier been characteristic of our poetry, remains.

The poetry of the later nineteenth century is not confined to the pre-Raphaelites, or to the romantic tradition.[2] Coventry Patmore in *The Angel in the House*, and in *The Unknown Eros*, broke with the prevailing fashion, both in diction and theme. In *The Angel in the House* he rediscovered a vocabulary for the narration of ordinary incident, and added to it a subtle, though apparently simple, diction for the exploration of philosophical and religious commentary. In *The Unknown Eros* he worked out an individual language more successfully than any poet since the seventeenth century, for the poetic record of religious experience. In the contemporary attack against so much in the past

[1] See p. 1.
[2] I have dealt with the poets mentioned in these paragraphs more fully in *English Poetry in the Later Nineteenth Century* (1933).

of our poetry his name is often forgotten, yet by comparison with his own century at least he is a major poet. For Patmore many of the problems which face his contemporaries do not exist. The world from which his verse arises is a world already made secure by his faith.

In more aggressive revolt against the prevailing romanticism was Thomas Hardy, who, in *The Dynasts*, missed only by a little bringing verse back to the stage, and brought it back successfully to a drama of the mind. In his lyrics he contrived to convey human actions, with new angles of vision in a vocabulary from which rhetoric and decorative phrasing had been removed. If Patmore created poetry within the experience of a Catholic, Hardy showed that a realism which was comfortless could still explore life, discovering at his best 'vivid and unique form'.[1] Further, whatever may be the assessment of Meredith as a poet, and judgments are bound to vary widely, it must be allowed that he broke with the prevailing romanticism. The early lyric of *Love in a Valley* may depend on melody but as one moves from *Modern Love* into the verbal thickets of the 'Earth' poems, a fresh approach in form and diction is almost painfully obvious.

If justice is to be done it must be admitted that while the nineteenth century did develop among its minor writers a romanticism which was sterile, it contained within itself the reaction. The followers of Swinburne, such as O'Shaughnessy, had developed an 'inane phraseology' with a vocabulary specialized, falsely artificial, more dead than that of the weakest imitator of Pope. Antagonism against such verse has spoilt our appreciation of the best things within that tradition from

[1] Lascelles Abercrombie in *Thomas Hardy* (1912).

Tennyson to Dowson. Further, it has led to a general depreciation of verse which is ornate, emblazoned. The modern poet, faced with later nineteenth-century romanticism, feels convinced that 'we shall not get any new efflorescence of verse until we get a new technique'. He is anxious not, as English poets have often been, to modify the past but to break with the past. This sense of irritation is not confined to the inadequacies of minor writers, but extends into an onslaught upon a whole century of verse. There has been a failure to remember that the romanticism of the later nineteenth century had ceased to identify itself with the purposes of Wordsworth or Coleridge or Shelley. Further, it has led much modern verse to place an aggressive importance on technique, which arises not wholly from the poet's own necessities, but from a desire to use a novel technique as a weapon against romanticism. Verse shall be made as intricate as possible, or alternatively as crude as possible, to defeat the lazy luxury of romantic vocabulary. A precedent for such practice was found in Donne, and another in Browning, but it has been employed with an added wilfulness in the erection of a vocabulary which is only privately intelligible. An early example is found in Meredith's philosophical poems where the diction is often individual, unexplained and deliberately uncouth. It always conceals a meaning, though that can only be discovered by the notes which the poet gave to a commentator.

Before the twentieth-century reaction set in there developed, with its final expression in the eighteen-nineties ,a last phase of romanticism, more compact than anything which had preceded it. Walter Pater's *Conclusion* of *Studies in the Renaissance* was the testament;

Wilde, the propagandist; Beardsley, the pictorial artist; and Ernest Dowson the poet. Even more precisely than with Swinburne the indebtedness was to French verse, particularly to Verlaine, modified by the influence of the Latin lyric of Horace and Propertius. Dowson had removed from poetry all its rhetoric; he had equally excluded all the problems which had occupied the endless controversies of the nineteenth century on religion and science. He had narrowed poetry to the small circle of his own sensations exquisitely expressed. Yet he retained the romantic approach, and used the old symbols of the rose, the vine, and the moon profusely almost as if he knew that they would not be needed again:

> We fling up flowers and laugh, we laugh across the wine;
>   With wine we dull our souls and careful strains of art;
> Our cups are polished skulls round which the roses twine:
>   None dares to look at Death who leers and lurks apart.[1]

If other ways in poetry have for a time obscured the beauty of his verses, or of the tradition to which they belonged, the neglect cannot remain permanent. They, no less than Pater's criticism, similarly out-moded, must return in however modified a form to affect once again the imagination of some 'maker'.

[1] *Carthusians.*

XIII

TOWARDS THE TWENTIETH CENTURY: GERARD MANLEY HOPKINS AND T. S. ELIOT

THE contemporary poet is in a situation which parallels in some ways that of Dryden. A war separates him from the ways of thought of an earlier generation; he is conscious that poetry has been reformed, and proud in a knowledge of the material world and of the workings of the mind itself superior to that possessed by his predecessors. In one important particular the comparison with Dryden will not hold. For Dryden, while he saw the difference between the literature before the Civil Wars and that of his own age, admired the 'giants before the flood'. Contemporary comment, beginning with dispraise of nineteenth-century poets, has often carried the disparagement against other writers in the past. Whatever the stature of a poet he can only achieve what there is in him to achieve, his verse seeming often to contradict the conclusions of his intellect, or to be in contrast to his temperament as this appears in his other activities. So William Morris, who had such gusto in his life, often writes dreamy and intangible verses. In our own age T. S. Eliot, who in his prose has advocated tradition, has in his poetry been more responsible than any other writer for the break with the past. The poet may at times find a hostile attitude to the past necessary to effect his own purposes, as Wordsworth with the 'gothic tales', or Keats with Pope. This seems to be the condition of some poets in the twentieth century.

It is far wiser to accept the criticism of poets when they praise, than when they condemn. The best criticism comes from poets interpreting their predecessors in relation to their own work. When the poet condemns it is usually with a passionate assertion, arising from some necessity in the work which he is himself creating. As has already appeared, English criticism has been free on the whole from such violence as far as the greater poets are concerned. The exceptions have been noted, but even with them the condemnation concerns usually not the great in the past, but the lesser figures who have masqueraded themselves into greatness. Nor in the contemporary period has this practice of tolerance wholly disappeared. It is true that certain young writers, who have gained a spurious reputation from their attachment to a political ideology, have played a guerilla warfare with the dead, which is at best a one-sided game. This is not an unusual activity, as can be seen from Byron's *English Bards*. Whether these young writers develop into poets remains to be seen, the journey from *English Bards* to *Don Juan* is a long one. Whether they achieve this or not, their aggressive tactics in prose comment need not be mistaken for criticism, nor need we be called upon to sacrifice our past to satisfy the subjugation of poetry to some political creed, itself only half assimilated. Not that the tolerance which has so long been a characteristic of our criticism has been entirely lost, for nowhere, not even in Dryden, is there a more disengaged open-mindedness than in

W. B. Yeats, and it may be that posterity will judge this age in poetry more through W. B. Yeats than any other name.

With Gerard Manley Hopkins, and later with T. S. Eliot, the break with the nineteenth century declares itself with distinctness. Though they both in their time bring new ways into poetry, they have a degree of tolerance which is beyond that found in much contemporary comment. When their prose criticism is compared it can be seen, however, that Eliot has a certain mannerism in criticism which is preparing the way for dissension and disparagement. Hopkins's criticism is to be found mainly in his letters, and they are often reminiscent of the letters of Keats, not in their conclusions but in the continuous and intense investigations of the poet's aim. Hopkins may even have stretched tolerance too far, as Gray did, in his appreciation of the work of his friends. His mind seems too valuable an instrument to be engaged in the minute criticism of Canon Dixon's poetry, and though he and Robert Bridges gained much from their friendship, it is clear that Bridges had only a limited sympathy with what Hopkins was attempting. It is instructive for the historian of literature that the least tolerant letter in Hopkins's criticism is one in which he attempts to set out poets as belonging to different schools of poetry: 'This modern medieval school is descended from the Romantic School (Romantic is a bad word) of Keats, Leigh Hunt, Hood, indeed of Scott early in the century. That was one school.'[1] The letter is a long one, and is wholly made up of such generalizations, which it is

---

[1] *The Correspondence of Gerard Manley Hopkins*, ed. C. C. Abbott, 1935: the letter of 1 Dec., 1881.

strange to discover in such an acute mind. When he comments on individual poets he employs far greater understanding, discovering their separate virtue, and what he has found enjoyable within them. It must be remembered that he finds his own poetical intentions in sharp contrast with those of his contemporaries, particularly with the nineteenth-century romantics. This does not prevent him from making a judicial estimate of their technical achievement. He expresses what he has found unacceptable in their verses without disparagement or contempt. This is the more remarkable because he is separated from nearly all of them, not only by a division of poetical method but by a more profound conflict in belief. Hopkins, like Langland, with whom he has some superficial technical resemblances, is secure within a Catholic faith which his poetry must serve. His tolerance can be seen in his comments on Keats whose genius he described as 'so astonishing, unequalled at his age and scarcely surpassed at any that one may surmise whether if he had lived he would not have rivalled Shakespeare'.[1] His many references to Tennyson show his appreciation of his craftsmanship and his enjoyment of individual poems, and this is the more interesting for it is through Tennyson that he comes to distinguish his own contrasting methods in diction and theme. He may feel that imitation of Tennyson would be sterile, but this does not lead him to speak with disdain. Rather he looks upon Tennyson as Chaucer looked upon the *Roman de la Rose*: 'Come what may he will be one of our greatest poets.' With Browning he was more severe, but it must be remembered that, poetical considerations apart, there was much in Browning openly

[1] 13 June, 1878.

to wound his faith. Of Browning's poetry he writes to Robert Bridges: 'I greatly admire the touches and the details, but the general effect, the whole, offends me, I think it repulsive.'[1] The main reason for this distaste, as far as it was poetical, arose from Browning's wilful disregard for tradition. At the same time he finds that he does not share Coventry Patmore's contempt of Browning: 'I suppose I am more tolerant or more inclined to admire than he is, but in listening to him I had that malignant satisfaction which lies in hearing one's worst surmises confirmed.'[2] The general tolerance in Hopkins's opinions, his desire to discover all that is possible from the past, is accompanied not unnaturally with a modesty about his own achievement. His passages on his own verse would be a salutary lesson to much in contemporary comment, and might be read along with his praise and understanding of Milton's genius and skill in verse.

Hopkins's own statement on his achievement is a far truer summary than the exaggerated praise of some contemporary comment which has attempted to elevate him by reducing his predecessors. In one passage, addressed to Bridges, he detected at once his own virtues and deficiencies: 'No doubt my poetry errs on the side of oddness. I hope in time to have a more balanced and Miltonic style. But as air, melody, is what strikes me most of all in music and design in painting, so design, pattern or what I am in the habit of calling "inscape", is what I above all aim at in poetry. Now it is the virtue of design, pattern, or inscape to be distinctive and it is the vice of distinctiveness to become queer. This vice

[1] 16 September, 1881.
[2] 12 August, 1883.

I cannot have escaped.'[1] Hopkins was seeking a way from nineteenth-century romanticism to the older traditions in English poetry. Not that he wished his poetry to deal with the past, for he came to feel that much nineteenth-century verse had become petrified with antiquarianism: 'the poetical language of an age should be the current language heightened, to any degree heightened and unlike itself, but not (I mean normally: passing freaks and graces are another thing) an obsolete one. This is Shakespeare's and Milton's practice and the want of it will be fatal to Tennyson's *Idylls* and plays, to Swinburne, and perhaps to Morris.'[2]

There is little in Hopkins's verse or in his criticism that can be explained by the classical or romantic contrast. As has already been seen, he was in reaction against the romanticism of the later nineteenth century, but this did not mean that he was against the early nineteenth century, or that his own verse or his principles conform to any definition of 'classical'. He was an advocate of tradition, as is Eliot later, but it is difficult to see that his verse is traditional, in any meaning of the term that will easily admit of interpretation. He may seem to reach back towards Langland, but the verse itself is very unlike Langland's, and their relationship to their audience is very different. Langland was using a measure and a vocabulary which his audience would recognize as an accepted medium for poetry. Hopkins is driven to construct a vocabulary and a method which is so individual that it becomes almost a private language at times. This is not done for wantonness, but it is part of the increased self-consciousness of the poet, which

[1] 15 February, 1879.
[2] To Bridges, 14 August, 1879.

the modern poet finds it difficult to avoid. The study of Hopkins suggests that the poet's relationship to belief, and to a mythological world, is more fundamental than any 'classical' and 'romantic' contrast. For him, the issue of belief is settled, and he is firm in his Catholic faith.

Poetically the matter is not so simple. For Christianity has never yielded to the poet the world of mythology which Greece and Rome gave so generously. Had Langland's tradition continued, or had the native miracle and morality plays been refashioned by the genius of Shakespeare or Ben Jonson, there might have existed in England this missing element, a religious poetry which could work itself out in epic and tragedy, for these were the forms which Hopkins considered as the highest in poetry. Had our religious history been continuous, the content of our poetry would have been different. As it is, Milton makes the nearest approach to that religious poetry presented in action, but the Renaissance has intervened between Milton and Langland, and bitter disruptions in Christendom, to encumber him in his great task. Religious poetry, as Dryden foresaw, became more the poetry of the individual experience, introspective and contemplative; its natural forms were the lyric, or discursive poetry. Such it had already become with Donne, with Herbert and Vaughan. This interpretation of religion through the individual experience led naturally to the poetry of Wordsworth, and Shelley and Keats. They may disregard in varying degrees the orthodox tenets of a Christian faith, but they discover whatever they are to define as spiritual from their own intuitional contacts with the world. With such an assertion of his own personality, and an emphasis on the individuality of the experience, Hopkins is not concerned. In what is best in him he reaches out beyond the personal, to the dramatic narrative, as in *The Wreck of the Deutschland*. Even in the lyrics, where he is expressing his religious experience, it is something which he regards as common to any Catholic, not that isolated experience which Wordsworth presented. Yet he was conscious that in his own time in England his experience was not a common one. He was aware of how he contrasted with so much else in his age, particularly in the poetry of his age. While he was aware of a religious tradition, and he was seeking after a poetical tradition, he had something of the self-consciousness of the convert. This was emphasized by the great originality of his mind, not unaccompanied by an element of eccentricity. His values at least, were secure, and he knew that poetry could not substantiate the vaunting claims made for it by Shelley, nor could it regenerate the world as Arnold had hoped. He saw it first as an art, as his numerous comments on the technique of poetry show so admirably. For him the purpose of that art, apart from the delight in the practise of it, remained in rendering the experiences of the faith within which he lived.

No writer has presented the break with the nineteenth century more clearly than T. S. Eliot, though his own statements in criticism must be weighed in the reckoning rather than all that has been said or done under his influence. It would be difficult to recall a poet who has effected such a change of taste within his own lifetime, or a critic, since Johnson, who has been heard with such deference. He is an innovator who has used as his password 'tradition', and possibly it is his American origins which have made him more self-conscious and explicit in this matter of tradition, which earlier English poets had interpreted in a less formal and more instinctive way. In T. E. Hulme and Irving Babbitt he had models in criticism which might have led him to excessive statement. Hulme's importance as a critic, if this is to be assessed solely from his published work, has been exaggerated, but his downrightness has set the tone for much contemporary comment on literature. Babbitt's *Rousseau and Romanticism* obviously had a powerful effect on Eliot, and not unnaturally, for it is the first reasoned and philosophical attack on romanticism to appear in the English language. Unfortunately, the least worthy sections in Babbitt's volume were his references to English writers, which were frequently petulant and sometimes misinformed. Occasionally, Eliot has imitated Babbitt's manner and the similarity increases in his later volumes of criticism where, like Babbitt, he is maintaining a faith, though not the same faith. Passages such as Eliot's comment on Meredith are unfortunate: 'Meredith, beyond a few acute and pertly expressed observations of human nature, has only a rather cheap and shallow "philosophy of life" to offer, Hopkins has the dignity of the Church behind him, and is consequently in closer contact with reality.'[1] Such venomous thrusts are far less frequent than the casual reader of Eliot's criticism might imagine. Compared with his younger contemporaries he is tolerant, though he has given in some unhappy passages a model for summary condemnation, spoken with every appearance of judicial authority and of irrevocability.

However much his verse may seem to break with the past he has in his prose, on more than one occasion, emphasized tradition: 'No poet, no artist of any art has

[1] *After Strange Gods*, 1934.

his complete meaning alone. His significance, his appreciation, is the appreciation of his relation to the dead poets and artists.'[1] Nor must it be forgotten that he has brought back into more general appreciation writers and dramatists, known to the scholar, but beyond that neglected. The Jacobean dramatists, and the metaphysical poets, and some prose writers, such as Lancelot Andrewes, have so been served by him, and their work has entered into the contemporary imagination not least through Eliot's own poetry. He has been the most powerful influence in gaining a wider recognition for the work of Pope and Johnson, though the influence of their steady and measured lines is less to be found in his own poetry. No one who has studied his work can have failed to make adjustments in his own values, or in his interpretation of individual writers. Unfortunately, in his praise of one great writer there is often inserted a crabbed, dispiriting reference to another. In his *Homage to John Dryden* Eliot compares Dryden to Milton: 'For Dryden, with all his intellect, had a commonplace mind. His powers were, we believe, wider, but no greater, than Milton's; he was confined by boundaries as impassable, though less straight.' There is no open attack, but a quiet assumption that we will concur in a diminution of Milton's greatness, with, further, some hidden suggestion that unless we agree there is something opaque or disordered in our critical insight.

Of his verse it is dangerous as yet to speak, for his work as a poet is unfinished. Already it can be seen that his later verse is far removed from the intentions with which he began. *The Love Song of J. Alfred Prufrock* has little, or nothing, in common with *Murder in the*

[1] *The Sacred Wood*, 1920.

G. M. HOPKINS AND T. S. ELIOT

Cathedral. The earliest poems are pre-war, and like Wordsworth's contributions to *Lyrical Ballads* they have attracted more attention than they merit, partly because they challenged attention in such an aggressive way. In some of those early verses Eliot used his technical skill, not for its own sake, or for the theme, but as a weapon of attack against the romanticism which preceded him. The poems themselves were not only poems but a satirical commentary on the prevailing fashions in poetry. Yet in some of those early poems his own underlying attitude was romantic, and in a sense of the term which in his prose criticism he would have condemned. For he was contrasting the inadequacy of contemporary life with some dreamland made out of phantasies of past beauty.

> I have heard the mermaids singing, each to each.
> I do not think that they will sing to me.

Byron, who sometimes saw life as a 'lazar-house of human woes', would have understood this disgust, though he would have been less patient of Eliot's fretful contemplation of his own misery. Even as late as *Burbank with a Baedeker* Eliot is exploring a romantic *malaise*, in the difference between the post-war world, and some belief in the experiences which were once possible. As far as the central underlying emotion is concerned, there is little that is new in the early verses: in part it is the mood of Byron, but still more that of Matthew Arnold.

The novelty lies not in the central emotion but in what Eliot himself has named the 'objective correlative'. The passage, which occurs in his essay on *Hamlet*, is among the most suggestive in his criticism: 'the only way of expressing emotion in the form of art is by finding an "objective correlative", in other words a set of objects, a situation, a chain of events, which shall be the formula of that *particular* emotion; such that when the eternal facts, which must terminate in sensory experience, are given, the emotion is immediately evoked.' Rossetti's *Burden of Nineveh*, Arnold's *Forsaken Merman* and *Burbank with a Baedeker*, all arise from a similar type of emotion. In all of them the poet is aware of inadequacy in contemporary experience as compared with the magnificence or appeal of some moment in the past or in the world of fabled things. But with Eliot the 'objective correlative' is different. Instead of portraying the beauty of some lovely and antique world, Eliot, to mask his discontent, gives a satiric picture of contemporary life, and contrasts it, sometimes regretfully, but more often cynically, with departed splendours.

The emphasis passes from the emotion itself to its expression, reversing the conclusion which Wordsworth had reached in his preface to the *Lyrical Ballads*. With Donne as his main example Eliot had revived a poetical vocabulary which would have the appearance of colloquial language and a natural rhythm. But in contrast to the apparent simplicity of the diction, and mocking it, as it were, he employed a quick, elliptical expression and an imagery newly minted and modern in its reference. The ear might receive the words and the movement of the verse easily, but the mind was held alert and taut. The sources of this language have often been investigated with the result that justice to its originality has seldom been fully conceded. Eliot knew Donne, and the Jacobean dramatists, Webster and Tourneur particularly, and obviously he had studied

Mallarmé, and Laforgue. But influences have been overstressed, for this language of wit, where the intellect keeps crowding out the lyric poet who is ever at hand if wanted, is an original and individual medium. In contrast to the earlier 'metaphysical' poets Eliot is far more self-conscious of the effects that he is making. He has assimilated some of the modern psychological studies, and by abandoning a logical sequence in his verse he attempts to make his lines image the very quick and wayward movement of a mind in action.

The development of Eliot as a poet is marked by the increasing importance of the subject in his verse, while he maintains a maturing control upon his technique. The stages from the early verse can be marked by *Gerontion*, *The Waste Land*, and *The Hollow Men*. In *Gerontion*, in his image of the old man, he discovered the exact dramatic theme for the personal emotion which had dominated the early verses. Then liberated from himself he attempted to elicit a poetic image of the distress of modern civilization, nor can any poet of our time stand in comparison with him in this hazardous attempt. His prose criticism shows how he valued such a theme in contrast with the expression of a personal emotion, and the change, not always noted, is his movement from a romantic to a classical conception of subject. The reference in *The Waste Land* is not to the individual but to the whole contemporary life of Western man. As far as theme is concerned, it is a return to Pope's way, though Pope is limited to man in his relationship with society, while in Eliot's poem, without any assertion of belief, there exists the consciousness of man as a spiritual being.

The difficulty in any such poem must rest primarily with the fable, or the incidents through which it can be recorded. That problem, if my assessment has been just, has been the concern of powerful poetical minds since the seventeenth century. Dryden, had he wished to solve Eliot's problem, would have had recourse to epic poetry, though, as has appeared, he found that he could not proceed beyond the discussion of the project. Eliot has no traditional mythology, no widely known group of fables which he shares with his reader, and can use as centres of reference. He has to create 'a heap of broken images' from Jessie L. Weston's *From Ritual to Romance*, from Frazer's *The Golden Bough*, from the *Upanishads* and a number of other sources. The poem may be enjoyed without an awareness of these sources, but it cannot be interpreted unless they are understood. Some critics have condemned Eliot for a wilfulness in this creation of symbols, without suggesting any possible alternative. Already, when Arnold was writing in 1865, the command to return to classical fable seemed mechanical and inapt; nor could the poet be any longer certain that a classical theme would be intelligible to a wide audience. Eliot is not attempting to create a secret language, as some of his contemporaries have done, for his own criticism shows that he desires to communicate with the reader and that he realizes the value of some myth or fable for that end: 'In using the myth,' he wrote of Joyce's *Ulysses*, 'in manipulating a continuous parallel between contemporaneity and antiquity, Mr. Joyce is pursuing a method which others must pursue after him. . . . It is simply a way of controlling, of ordering, of giving a shape and a significance to the immense panorama of futility and anarchy which is contemporary history. It is a method already adumbrated by Mr. Yeats, and of the need for which I believe

Mr. Yeats to have been the first contemporary to be conscious.'[1] In *The Waste Land*, Eliot has made his symbolism out of fragments many of them unfamiliar, and none with the same degree of intelligibility as a traditional fable or mythology. It may be that nothing in the past matched his purposes, for he cannot be suspected here, as in some of the earlier poems, of delighting in obscurity for its own sake. In his later verse, after the consummation of this middle period with *The Hollow Men*, Eliot has turned to Christian themes, and to dramatic verse. As with Shelley, the application of verse to drama has brought inevitably a greater simplicity into its texture: also it has brought intelligibility. *The Journey of the Magi* and *Murder in the Cathedral* may mark the beginning in Eliot of a new poetry, though it is difficult to see that as works of art they have strength comparable with *The Waste Land*, and *The Hollow Men*.

Eliot has spoken of 'tradition' more often perhaps than any other poet in England. In this it must not be forgotten, as already emphasized, that he is an American by birth and more accustomed to a written constitution than to judgments from precedent. English writers, and the greater English poets, have valued the past without having to speak too vehemently about it. Eliot's verse, like that of Wordsworth, refuses to be held in by the prescriptions of his prose criticism. Much in it grew out of his antagonism to the poetry that immediately preceded him. Some reaction against the romanticism of the nineteenth century was inevitable, and in its time salutary. In another and more subtle way, and against

[1] *The Dial*, November, 1923, quoted, F. O. Matthiessen, *The Achievement of T. S. Eliot*, 1935.

his own will, possibly, he has helped to destroy the sense of tradition. Every reader of his verse will recall his device of inserting into his own lines a complex and interesting reference or phrase from older writers. This practice of allusiveness is not new in poetry, but Eliot's way of manipulating it is different from that of any English writer. When Milton captures a Virgilian phrase into his verse, the reader who recalls the original will return to it with some additional pleasure. For in employing the phrase Milton interprets it in such a way that its original meaning is left, certainly undamaged and often enhanced. Eliot, on the other hand, employs lines from older poetry savagely, satirically, so that the magnificence of the original passage is torn down and trampled, and all that our contemporary confusion may be more clearly displayed. As the Freudian child wishes to murder his father, so often the modern poet wishes to murder the past, and wherever he discovers beauty therein, or magnificence, to ravage and destroy it. The most deliberte example is in 'A Game of Chess' in *The Waste Land*, and very effectively is the contrast manipulated. A more obvious instance is in *Burbank with a Baedaker*:

> The horses, under the axletree
>   Beat up the dawn from Istria
> With even feet. Her shuttered barge
>   Burned on the water all the day.
>
> But this or such was Bleistein's way:
>   A saggy bending of the knees
> And elbows, with the palms turned out,
>   Chicago Semite Viennese.

Eliot is not respecting the past, or manipulating it, but devouring it.

XIV

W. B. YEATS AND THE CONTINUANCE OF TRADITION

THROUGHOUT this study, from Chaucer onwards, it has appeared that in English verse a certain compromise between extreme doctrines has existed. Further, that while 'romanticism' has never reached in England the same precise and emphatic definition as in France and Germany, elements of 'romanticism' have been found in English poetry over a longer period and in more varied ways than elsewhere. For the very reason that the 'romantic' has been mixed and diluted in England, there has been possible a marked continuity of tradition. Such an assertion need not obscure the changes which have come over the nature of poetry, but these arise from changes in mental environment and social circumstance. They are inevitable, therefore, and not manufactured to defend a 'school' or support a programme. Nor have the greatest of our poets looked upon their predecessors with bitterness: Dryden and W. B. Yeats can both compare Chaucer's poetry with their own, each knowing the inevitable differences, but both conscious of what Chaucer achieved. The historians of literature have helped with their vitiating vocabulary of 'schools' and 'periods', to emphasize distinctions which are sometimes non-existent, and seldom operate as they would have us believe. Chaucer did not know that he lived in 'the dawn of the Renaissance', and Gray would have been surprised and probably severely displeased to hear that he was a 'pre-romantic'. Poetry—and the malicious will rejoice to find such a comment at the end of a work such as this—has suffered more than any of the arts from an excess of criticism. Above all, it has had to endure the activities of a categorizing mind. The only satisfactory criticism is not of an age or of a period, but of a single work of art, studied in relationship to all that is relevant for its interpretation. So studied, the minor writers, out of whom the 'periods' and 'schools' are often manufactured, sink to their proper place.

In the contemporary period, criticism has often spoken with harshness; many a great name has been referred to with disparagement, and the contrast of 'classical' and 'romantic' has been resurrected in order to condemn, under the name of a formula, elements which in some form or another have always been present in English verse. Against all this Yeats stood in contrast. He has himself confessed to the romanticism of his earlier years: 'I was in all things Pre-Raphaelite.'[1] Nor did he ever regret the decorative grace of his early lyrics. He knew that a poem such as *The Lake Isle of Innisfree* had been too often heard, and imitated, so that it had grown stale, like a fashion shared by everybody:

> But the fools caught it,
> Wore it in the world's eyes
> As though they'd wrought it.
> Song, let them take it,
> For there's more enterprise
> In walking naked.

[1] *Four Years* (1921).

He realized, no one better, that verse must take to new ways, and Paddington Railway Station became a theme for verse instead of Tristram and Iseult. But very much as Chaucer had done, he looked with respect on what had been abandoned. He came in those four volumes, *The Wild Swans at Coole*, *Michael Robartes and the Dancer*, *The Tower*, and *The Winding Stair*, to a verse, bare, taut, austere, but beautiful, with a beauty purified:

> Though the great song return no more
> There's keen delight in what we have:
> The rattle of pebbles on the shore
> Under the receding wave.

In one of his comments on verse he defined the antagonism between the poet and his world as rhetoric, and between the poet and himself as poetry. So in his own work he will not permit argument to replace vision. It is true that in this he has a degree of self-consciousness which modern poetry can seldom avoid. One may sometimes suspect that he would have preferred to be a poet in the days when Christendom was united: 'Morris had never seemed to care for any poet later than Chaucer; and though I preferred Shakespeare to Chaucer I begrudged my own preference. Had not Europe shared one mind and heart, until both mind and heart began to break into fragments a little before Shakespeare's birth?'[1] The problem of belief, and of some fable or mythology adequate for his purposes, the two recurring problems which face the poet, possessed him as they had done Milton, Dryden, Blake and so

[1] *Four Years* (1921).

many others. His solution was individual and, like so much else in his work, seems to combine a number of loyalties from the past. He found that he had to create his symbols but more than once he suggests that he would have been happier to find them in some established tradition. He seems to be thinking of himself when he writes of Blake: 'he was a man crying out for a mythology, and trying to make one because he could not find one to his hand. Had he been a Catholic of Dante's time he would have been well content with Mary and the angels.'[1] His own attempts to build up a mythology are at times a little self-conscious, but when his imagery is only dimly intelligible the verse has such mastery, that the poems can be accepted as music is accepted.

In so constructing a group of symbols, he was influenced by Blake and Shelley. In his prose he has made statements about the nature of experience as mystical as anything in Blake, and he has made claims for the potency of poetry which transcend anything in Shelley's work. So in his essay on *The Symbolism of Poetry* he writes: 'I am certainly never certain, when I hear of some war, or of some religious excitement or of some new manufacture, or of anything else that fills the ear of the world, that it has not all happened because of something that a boy piped in Thessaly.' This boldness of assertion is not linked, as it is in Blake and Shelley, with a reforming zeal. Always his mysticism seems well under control, as if it were something which he knew to be good for his poetry, and in his later verse it is combined with an economy of expression, of bareness and strength, comparable to the prose of Swift. This control of the medium, always secure, was sometimes

[1] *Ideas of Good and Evil.*

audacious, as if he picked up simple words at random and, without changing their order or their meaning, set them casually into his verses, only to discover that they had acquired a rugged power, or a strange and intangible beauty.

Blake's art becomes obscure from the very pressure and originality of his vision, but with Yeats the poet remains in control. At times this impression is so strong that Yeats seems to remain in a position similar to that of Rossetti or the early Swinburne of cultivating art for its own sake. His language in his essays is sometimes reminiscent of the early letters of Keats. Yet he had always the belief that while poetry was a craft it was also part of a secret wisdom. The poet, through his symbols, might disclose this ancient and hidden revelation. To this idea Yeats frequently recurs, never more impressively than in the conclusion of his essay on *The Philosophy of Shelley's Poetry*: 'there is for every man some one scene, some one adventure, some one picture that is the image of his secret life, for wisdom first speaks in images, and this one image . . . would lead his soul, disentangled from unmeaning circumstance and the ebb and flow of the world, into that far household, where the undying gods await all whose souls have become simple as flame, whose bodies have become quiet as an agate lamp.'

His verse derives from a wider experience than that of any of the Pre-Raphaelites or of Keats. If his attempt to build a new Irish drama and a new Irish folk-literature may seem at times a little unreal, it is because it can now be seen in comparison with the later verse. His tragic experiences in the Easter Rebellion and in the events of the Civil War give to some of his later poems the sense of an experience highly individual and yet intelligible from its wide contacts with common humanity. To the last much in his verse is drawn from the elements that have been called romantic at one time or another in English poetry, but they have at their centre this continuous contact with the normal. In this union of opposite qualities the distinctive and most valuable features of his later verse can be found.

The profession of poetry may become increasingly difficult, and Yeats's self-consciousness is an indication that he himself found this in his relation with the modern world. With all his contemplation of the possible themes for poetry he never discovered his way to a poem of action, or to a poem as wide in its contemporary reference as *The Waste Land*. He remained with his images and his symbols in that bare lyrical beauty which still haunts us so strongly that we are unable to see what it omits. It exists rather as the individual vision than as a general human vision, yet ever his mind, even when most aloof, is reaching out towards traditional wisdom. But in the quest of traditional elements he becomes continuously aware of some antagonism between the poet and contemporary society, and the dominant ways of thought. Such a conclusion recurs frequently in his prose: 'I am very religious, and deprived by Huxley and Tyndall, whom I detested, of the simple-minded religion of my childhood, I had made a new religion, almost an infallible church out of poetic tradition: a fardel of stories, and of personages, and of emotions, a bundle of images, and of masks, passed from one generation to another, by poets and painters, with some help from philosophers and theologians . . . I had even created a dogma: "Because those imaginary people are created out of the deepest instinct of man, to be his measure and his norm, whatever I can imagine those mouths speaking may be the nearest I can go to truth.'"[1]

The traditional becomes involved at times in a secret language, a hidden reference, which was not necessary for Chaucer, or Shakespeare or Milton. He is aware that the merchant and the Puritan have, together with the materialist, produced a view of the world in which the poet can only function with difficulty: 'Puritanism... had denied the sacredness of an earth that commerce was about to corrupt and ravish.'[2] 'The hurried and successful' nations had lost vision, and even the 'greatest poets see the world with preoccupied minds'. It was for this reason that Yeats, in an age which had disparaged so much in the past, looked back to earlier times determined that nothing valuable in the tradition of poetry should be lost. On one occasion he described how he had been reading Boccaccio and Cervantes and come to feel that they belonged to the same world: 'It is we who are different.' He attempted to explain that difference by the intrusion of 'the newspapers, all kinds of second-rate books, the preoccupation of men with all kinds of practical changes', which 'have driven the living imagination out of the world'. Boccaccio and Cervantes 'had not to deal with the world in such great masses that it could only be represented to their minds by figures and by abstract generalizations. Everything that their minds ran on came to them vivid with the colour of the senses, and when they wrote it was out of their own rich experience, and they found their

[1] *Four Years*, 1921.
[2] *Edmund Spenser*.

symbols of expression in things that they had known all their life long'. In Yeats himself, despite the difficulties, experience never degenerated into habit, and this was possible mainly because he was strengthened by this generous understanding of the past. The profession of poetry may become still increasingly difficult, in an age that, unlike that of Yeats, has no memories of a pre-war world. While poetry cannot exist solely in the past, or in its memory, the long tradition of our verse, and the sense of its continuous development, increases in importance. At no time can we afford less to destroy for the sake of a critical formula, or a political creed, what we have inherited.

INDEX

Abbott, C. C., 187.
Abercrombie, Lascelles, 182.
Addison, Joseph, 10, 86, 94, 178.
Æschylus, 147, 148.
Allen, B. Sprague, 77.
Aquinas, St. Thomas, 47.
Ariosto, 30, 76, 142.
Aristotle, 43, 100.
Arnold, Matthew, 97, 130, 132, 137, 149, 156, 157, 159, 172–179, 195, 196.

Babbitt, Irving, 2, 21, 193.
Bacon, Francis, 15, 34–37, 105, 142.
Bagehot, Walter, 157, 166.
Balzac, Honoré, 166.
Barbauld, Mrs. A. L., 118.
Baudelaire, Charles, 4, 131, 179.
Beardsley, Aubrey, 184.
Beaumont, Élie, de, 86.
Beckford, William, 81–82, 88.
Blake, William, 98, 99–108, 126, 145, 151, 177, 203, 204, 205.
Boccaccio, 23, 25, 207.
Boehme, Jacob, 102
Boethius, 26.
Boileau, 18, 19, 20, 63, 66, 69–70.
Borel, Pétrus, 181.
Bossu, René le, 61, 62.
Bottrall, R., 116–117.
Bowles, W. L., 12, 87, 116.
Bridges, Robert, 4, 187–192.

Browning, Robert, 4, 17, 136, 165–171, 173, 188, 189.
Brunetière, Ferdinand, 13.
Buck, Samuel, 77–78, 124.
Burke, Edmund, 57.
Bush, Douglas, 37, 48, 122, 131, 144, 169.
Butts, Thomas, 101.
Byron, George Gordon, Lord, 12, 14, 60, 71, 85, 103, 109–128, 132, 137, 156, 169, 178, 179, 186, 195.

Calderon, 141.
Campbell, Thomas, 114.
Campion, Edmund, 177.
Carew, Thomas, 44–45.
Carlyle, Thomas, 159.
Carter, Elizabeth, 79–80.
Cervantes, 207.
Chambers, Sir E. K., 120.
Chambers, Sir William, 87.
Chapman, George, 17.
Chapman, Guy, 81.
Chatterton, Thomas, 96.
Chaucer, Geoffrey, 4, 20, 22, 23–43, 62, 63, 85, 89, 91, 158, 161, 164, 167, 168, 174, 177, 180, 188, 201, 202, 203, 207.
Claude, 78.
Climenson, E. J., 79.
Coleridge, S. T., 4, 5, 14, 15, 18, 29, 40–42, 88, 95, 97, 109–128 131, 142, 183.

Collins, William, 91, 97.
Courthope, W. J., 72, 113.
Cowley, Abraham, 47–53, 109.
Cowper, William, 113, 122, 127.
Crabbe, George, 115.

Dante, 13, 29, 46, 107, 146, 154, 160, 162, 204.
Davenant, Sir William, 51–55, 65.
Deane, C. V., 124.
Dennis, John, 65.
Despencer, Lord de, 79.
Dickens, Charles, 166.
Dixon, R. W., 187–192.
Dodington, Rt. Hon. George, 79.
Donne, John, 44–49, 53, 57, 65, 68, 76, 122, 127, 160, 166, 171, 174, 183, 191, 196.
Doren, Mark van, 18.
Dover, Lord, 84.
Dowson, Ernest, 183, 184.
Drayton, Michael, 177.
Dryden, John, 4, 18, 29, 45, 58, 60, 61–70, 88, 91, 101, 122, 125, 161, 174, 185, 186, 194, 198, 201, 203.
Duckworth, F. R. G., 166.
Dyott, Sir William, 68.
Eckermann, J. P., 11.
Eliot, T. S., 2, 3, 67, 159, 185, 187, 191, 192–200.
Ellis-Fermor, V. M., 40.
Evelyn, John, 9.
Fielding, Henry, 157.
Fillmore, J. C., 16.
Fontenelle, 8.
Forman, H. Buxton, 154.
Forman, M. Buxton, 132.

Foster, John, 15.
Frazer, Sir James, 198.
Froissart, 100.

Gautier, Théophile, 131, 179.
Gibbs, James, 77.
Gillies, R. P., 85.
Godwin, William, 20, 104, 147, 148.
Goethe, 11, 12, 13, 17.
Goldsmith, Oliver, 75.
Gotthard, H., 9.
Gray, Thomas, 10, 97, 99–108, 113, 174, 187, 202.
Grierson, Sir Herbert, 58.
Griggs, E. L., 112.

Hall, John, 18.
Hardy, Thomas, 182.
Harvey, Gabriel, 29.
Hawksmoor, Nicholas, 77.
Hazlitt, William, 88, 129.
Heine, 10.
Herbert, George, 191.
Herodotus, 100, 141.
Hill, Aaron, 68.
Hobbes, Thomas, 9, 15, 50–55, 63.
Hodgson, Francis, 113.
Holinshed, Raphael, 38.
Homer, 17, 42, 66, 68, 72, 88, 141, 142, 162.
Hood, Thomas, 187.
Hopkins, G. M., 4, 159, 185–192.
Horace, 18, 19, 69, 72, 100, 131, 184.
Housman, A. E., 3, 178.
Hugo, Victor, 12.
Hulme, T. E., 1, 21, 193.
Hunt, Leigh, 135, 187.

INDEX

Hurd, Richard, 9, 11.
Hussey, Christopher, 90.
Huxley, Thomas, 206.

James, D. G., 120.
James, Henry, 165.
Jeffrey, R. W., 68.
Johnson, Samuel, 18, 41, 61, 66, 74, 75, 86, 87, 94, 106, 113, 174, 194.
Jones, R. F., 47.
Jonson, Ben, 17, 19, 42, 2, 177, 191.
Joyce, James, 198.
Juvenal, 18.

Keats, John, 45, 58, 66, 68, 88, 95, 98, 99, 123, 129-138, 139, 148, 156, 160, 162, 163, 165, 166, 168, 173, 179, 180, 187, 191, 205.
Ker, W. P., 12, 15, 24, 77, 78, 104, 154, 155, 165, 174.
Kind, J. L., 94.

Laforgue, Jules, 197.
Landor, W. S., 17.
Langland, William, 28-29, 31, 33, 150, 177, 188, 190, 191.
Lavater, J. K., 102.
Lessing, G. E., 90.
Lewis, C. S., 30, 32.
Lewis, [Monk], 111.
Livy, 107.
Locke, John, 9. 20, 78, 105, 123.
'Longinus', 18.
Lowes, J. L., 25-26.
Lucas, F. L., 1.
Lucretius, 154.

Macaulay, T. B., 159.
Macpherson, James, 88, 96, 105, 112-3.
Mallarmé, Stéphane, 197.
Marmontel, 72.
Mathiessen, F. O., 199.
Medwin, Thomas, 144.
Meredith, George, 27, 183, 193.
Millican, C. B., 32.
Milton, John, 17, 29, 37, 53-60, 68, 70, 74, 85, 86, 89, 91, 93, 95, 110, 117, 122, 127, 129, 130, 131, 134, 139, 146, 148, 151, 157, 160, 161, 163, 189, 190, 191, 194, 200.
Moore, Thomas, 114, 116.
More, J., 89.
Morley, Edith, 94, 103.
Morris, William, 179, 180, 181, 185.
Murray, John, 115.
Musset, Alfred de, 7.

Newton, Sir Isaac, 105.
North, Sir Thomas, 38.

O'Shaughnessy, Arthur, 182.
Ovid, 62.
Owen, Wilfred, 4.
Owst, G. B., 29.

Pascal, 2.
Pater, Walter, 97, 183, 184.
Patmore, Coventry, 181-182, 189.
Peacock, T. L., 139, 141, 142, 143.
Péladan, Josephan, 181.
Pepys, Samuel, 9.
Percy, Thomas, 96, 109.

Perrault, Charles, 8.
Petrarch, 45.
Philips, Ambrose, 71.
Plato, 103, 141, 142.
Plautus, 18.
Plutarch, 38.
Poe, E. A., 21.
Pope, Alexander, 4, 18, 45, 67–75, 76, 86, 88, 93, 94, 101, 110, 113, 114, 115, 116, 120, 123, 126, 127, 129, 136, 157, 161, 164, 174, 178, 194, 197.
Pound, Ezra, 4.
Praz, Mario, 1, 21, 81, 181.
Powys, Mrs. P. L., 79.
Prior, Mathew, 113.
Propertius, 184.
Pulci, 116.

Racine, 59.
Radcliffe, Mrs. Ann, 112.
Raleigh, Sir Walter, 29.
Rapin, Réne, 62.
Read, Herbert, 2, 4.
Rennes, J. J. van, 87–88.
Renwick, W. L., 32.
Reynolds, Sir Joshua, 92, 101.
Richards, I. A., 101, 120.
Richardson, Samuel, 68, 157.
Rimbaud, J. A., 21.
Robertson, J. G., 7.
Robinson, Henry Crabb, 103.
Rogers, Samuel, 68, 115.
Rosa, Salvator, 78.
Rossetti, D. G., 5, 179, 180, 196, 205.
Rousseau, J. J., 1, 20, 79, 100, 124.
Rowe, Nicholas, 100.
Ruskin, John, 169.

Rymer, Thomas, 62.

Saintsbury, G., 91–93.
Sandys, George, 48.
Santayana, George, 146, 154.
Schlegel, A. W., 12.
Schiller, J. C. F., 12.
Scott, Sir Walter, 56, 67, 85, 96, 99, 109–128, 157, 187.
Seneca, 18.
Shaftesbury, Earl of, 10, 72.
Shakespeare, William, 7, 18, 19, 25, 27, 33, 34, 37–43, 44, 53, 57, 62, 68, 84, 86, 89, 93, 100, 129, 134, 135, 136, 137, 153, 157, 160, 162, 165, 167, 171, 177, 188, 190, 203, 207.
Shawcross, John, 120, 142.
Shelley, P. B., 15, 17, 66, 70, 85, 86, 88, 98, 102, 103, 104, 117, 121, 123, 134, 139–155, 156, 160, 163, 164, 173, 177, 183, 191, 192, 204, 205.
Sidney, Sir Philip, 70, 142, 199.
Smart, Christopher, 97.
Smith, D. Nichol, 92.
Smith, L. P., 9, 12.
Soames, Sir William, 63, 69.
Southey, Robert, 144.
Spens, Janet, 30, 33.
Spenser, Edmund, 14, 20, 28–43, 45, 48, 57, 60, 61, 70, 89, 93, 117, 123, 129, 130, 170, 180, 207.
Spindler, R., 165.
Sprat, T., 9.
Staël, Madame de, 12, 114.
Steinke, M. W., 94, 95.
Stendahl, 12.
Stockdale, P., 87.

INDEX

Smith, Thomas, 107.
Strich, Franz, 13.
Swedenborg, Emmanuel, 103.
Swift, Jonathan, 8, 69, 71, 72, 94, 139, 204.
Swinburne, A. C., 17, 65, 131, 180, 181, 184.
Tasso, 30, 55.
Tennyson, Alfred, Lord, 17, 20, 27, 45, 156–165, 180, 188, 190.
Theocritus, 18.
Thomas, W., 94.
Thompson, Francis, 153.
Thomson, James, 75, 78, 89–92, 107, 114, 122, 124, 127.
Tillyard, E. M. W., 56, 59.
Toffanin, Giuseppe, 8.
Tooke, Andrew, 48, 149.
Tourneur, Cyril, 196.
Toynbee, Mrs. Paget, 83.
Tyndall, John, 206.

Ullman, R. 9.

Vaughan, Henry, 191.
Verlaine, Paul, 184.
Virgil, 65, 66, 152, 163.

Visiak, E. H., 59.
Voltaire, 20, 43, 59, 62.

Waller, Edmund, 52.
Walpole, Horace, 81, 82–86, 88, 95, 105, 106, 111.
Ward, T. W., 174, 176.
Warton, J., 91–98, 109.
Warton, T., 13, 91–98.
Webster, John, 196.
West, Richard, 100.
Weston, Jessie, L., 198.
Wilde, Oscar, 184.
Willey, Basil, 123.
Williams, G. J., 84.
Wordsworth, William, 4, 5, 14, 15, 18, 29, 58, 66, 70, 88, 95, 98, 102, 103, 104, 107, 109–128, 130, 131, 132, 134, 135, 139, 142, 150, 151, 156, 157, 158, 163, 164, 167, 168, 173, 179, 180, 183, 196, 199.

Yeats, W. B., 150, 187, 198, 201–208.
Young, Edward, 92–98, 109, 131.

For Product Safety Concerns and Information please contact our EU
representative GPSR@taylorandfrancis.com
Taylor & Francis Verlag GmbH, Kaufingerstraße 24, 80331 München, Germany

www.ingramcontent.com/pod-product-compliance
Lightning Source LLC
Chambersburg PA
CBHW052110300426
44116CB00010B/1604